# PHILIPPIANS
## *In the Greek New Testament*

WORD STUDIES IN
THE GREEK NEW TESTAMENT
*For the English Reader*

by Kenneth S. Wuest

1. GOLDEN NUGGETS FROM THE GREEK N. T.
2. BYPATHS IN THE GREEK N. T.
3. TREASURES FROM THE GREEK N. T.
4. UNTRANSLATABLE RICHES
5. PHILIPPIANS
6. FIRST PETER
7. GALATIANS
8. STUDIES IN VOCABULARY
9. HEBREWS
10. MARK
11. GREAT TRUTHS TO LIVE BY
12. THE PASTORIAL EPISTLES
13. EPHESIANS AND COLOSSIANS
14. IN THESE LAST DAYS
15. PROPHETIC LIGHT IN THE PRESENT DARKNESS
16. ROMANS

THE NEW TESTAMENT
IN EXPANDED TRANSLATION

# PHILIPPIANS

## *In the Greek New Testament*

### FOR THE ENGLISH READER

*by*

## KENNETH S. WUEST, LL.D.

**WM. B. EERDMANS PUBLISHING COMPANY**
Grand Rapids          Michigan

**PHILIPPIANS**
*by* KENNETH S. WUEST

*Copyright*, 1942, *by*
*Wm. B. Eerdmans Publishing Co.*

All rights in this book are reserved. No part may be reproduced
in any manner without permission in writing from the publisher,
except brief quotations used in connection with a review in a
magazine or newspaper.

ISBN 0-8028-1234-1

*Set up and printed, July 1942*
*Sixteenth reprinting, August 1978*

PHOTOLITHOPRINTED BY EERDMANS PRINTING COMPANY
GRAND RAPIDS, MICHIGAN, UNITED STATES OF AMERICA

## DEDICATED

To Wilbur M. Smith, D.D., colleague of mine on the Faculty of The Moody Bible Institute of Chicago, who has won my deep and abiding love by his devotion to the Lord Jesus; for whom I have the greatest admiration because of his sanctified scholarship and tireless energy in His service; whose genuine Christian friendship I treasure most highly; and to whom I am sincerely grateful for the encouragement he has given me in my work in the Greek New Testament.

# INTRODUCTION

E VERY book should have a reason for its existence. One hesi-
tates to add another volume to the many excellent works
written on Paul's letter to the Philippians. It would seem that
an author is justified in doing so however, providing he can offer
the Bible student a treatment of this epistle which is unique, and
which gives him an access to it which no other book offers. Greek
scholars write for the person who knows Greek. Here is a book
which offers to the Bible student who has no knowledge of
Greek, and who has had no formal training in Bible study, word
studies in 297 Greek words found in the Philippian epistle, presenting the material in such a simple easy-to-be-understood manner that he is able to enjoy some of the untranslatable richness of
the Greek New Testament, a thing heretofore denied him.

In addition to this help, a fresh translation of the entire epistle
is offered. This translation, used in connection with the English
reader's study Bible, will, together with the Greek word studies,
enable the student to arrive at a much clearer understanding of
his English text than he would otherwise be able to have, and also
make accessible to him a great deal of the richness of the Greek
text which does not at all appear in his English translation.

The word studies and the translation offered, represent many
hours of patient, exhausting, and careful research. The writer,
for the most part, has not included the intricate technicalities of
Greek grammar, syntax, and idiom in the presentation of the
material. He has not offered any explanation of certain interpre-

tations and translations simply because to do so would swamp the reader with detailed discussion involving technicalities in the Greek which the student of the English Bible would not understand. The translation offered must not be used as a substitute for the standard translations such as the Authorized Version, for instance, but as a companion translation which will help make clearer the standard version used. But this does not mean that the translation offered is a paraphrase, namely, a translation including explanatory or interpretive material. Just because a translator uses more words than the Authorized Version has, does not say that his translation is not accurate, nor does it imply that the Authorized Version is not dependable. It merely is indicative of the fact that the Greek language can say more in less words than the English, and that if one wants to bring over into the English translation more of the richness of the Greek, he will have to use more words, that is all. The words in parentheses are not part of the translation, but are explanatory.

Smoothness of diction and elegance of expression have been sacrificed in order to bring out more clearly the thought of the original. The usual English order of words has been set aside at times, so that the Greek order may be followed, for the Greek places his words in such a position in the sentence as will bring out emphasis where emphasis is desired. The author has tried to show connections more clearly, where these are obscured by the condensed literality of the standard translations. Finally, the translation in modern day English rather than in the polished periods of the Authorized Version, much of which we know by heart and love, is thought-provoking. Paul's letter divided into chapters and verses, furnished with footnotes, marginal readings, an introduction, and cross Scripture references becomes for the

Bible student, a Bible book to be studied as a religious treatise. And this is as it should be. But one misses the frank, intimate informality of the letter as seen when one reads it for what it is, a letter of a missionary to some of his converts, thanking them for a gift which they had sent him. And so, while the word studies and translation have been arranged according to verses for purposes of study, the entire translation has also been offered in the form of a letter. We have divided it into paragraphs in order that it might be more easily read, although letters of the first century do not appear to have been written in that way. Read it at a sitting, and catch the charm of this friendly, informal, "thank-you" letter, every word in its Greek original inspired by God, and thus the infallible Word of God, and yet full of the human writer, his style of writing, his character, and his personality.

Then, with all this fresh in your mind, begin a verse by verse study of the letter. With your standard translation open before you, read the first verse. Follow each word study, endeavoring to understand more clearly the translation which you are using. Then read the fuller translation which the author offers. Work slowly through the epistle in this way, and you will be gratified to find that you have come to a clearer understanding of one of the best loved Bible books, and that you have also made your own some of the untranslatable richness of the Greek text itself.

The work which the writer has done is chiefly interpretive, leaving for the Bible student the delightful exercise of developing, enlarging upon, and applying the truth brought out. The word studies rarely go afield, treatment of the Greek words found in this epistle being confined to the book itself. Where a word has been treated more fully, or completely, or in its every occurrence, or where the thought has been developed in the author's four other books, a footnote will direct the student to the page or pages where such treatment can be found. These books are *Golden Nuggets from the Greek New Testament for the English Reader*, *Bypaths in the Greek New Testament for the English Reader*, *Treasures from the Greek New Testament for the English Reader*, and *Untranslatable Riches from the Greek New Testament for the English Reader*. These books will be mentioned by the abbreviated titles of *Nuggets*, *Bypaths*, *Treasures*, and *Riches*.

# CONTENTS

# PHILIPPIANS

*In the Greek New Testament*

# Paul's Letter

*Paul and Timothy, bondslaves by nature, belonging to Christ Jesus, to all the consecrated and separated ones in Christ Jesus, together with the overseers and ministering deacons. (Sanctifying) grace be to you, and (heart) peace, from God our Father and from the Lord Jesus Christ.*

*I am thanking my God constantly for my whole remembrance of you, always in every prayer of mine making supplication for you all with joy. I am constantly thanking my God for your joint-participation in the furtherance of the gospel from the first day until this particular moment, having come to this settled and firm persuasion concerning this very thing, that He who began in you a work which is good, will bring it to a successful conclusion right up to the day of Christ Jesus; even as it is right for me to be constantly turning my mind in the direction of this very thing in your behalf (namely, the completion of God's good work in you), because you are holding me in your heart both in my bonds and in my defense and confirmation of the gospel, you all being co-sharers with me in this grace; for my witness is God, how I long after all of you with the tender-heartedness of Christ Jesus.*

*And this is the constant purport of my definite petitions, namely, that your love yet more and more may overflow, but at the same time be kept within the guiding limitations of an accurate knowledge gained by experience and those of every kind of sensitive moral and ethical tact, so that you may after testing, recognize the true value of the finer points of Christian conduct and thus sanction them, in order that you may be pure and not a stumbling block, keeping in view the day of Christ, being filled*

full with the fruit of righteousness, which fruit is through Jesus
Christ, resulting in glory and praise to God.

But after mature consideration I desire you to gain this knowledge from (my) experience, that my circumstances have come to
result rather in the pioneer advance of the gospel, so that it has
become plainly recognized that my bonds are because of Christ,
throughout the whole Praetorian Guard and to all the rest. And
the great majority of the brethren having come to a state of
settled confidence in the Lord by reason of the fact that they
have been persuaded by my bonds, are more abundantly bold,
fearlessly breaking their silence and speaking the Word. In fact,
certain ones even because of envy and rivalry, but also others
because of good will are proclaiming Christ; some indeed out
of a spirit of love, knowing that I am appointed for the defense
of the gospel; but others out of a partisan self-seeking spirit are
announcing Christ, not with pure unmixed motives, but insincerely, thinking to make my chain gall me.

What is my feeling in view of these things? (Supposing they
do purpose to make my chain gall me.) The only thing that
follows is that in every manner whether in pretense or in truth,
whether insincerely or sincerely, Christ is being announced; and
in this I am rejoicing, and certainly I will continue to rejoice,
for I know that this for me shall result in salvation through your
petition and through the bountiful supply of the Spirit of Jesus
Christ. And this is exactly in accordance with my undivided and
intense expectancy and hope, namely, that in respect to not even
one thing shall I be ashamed, but in every boldness of speech as
always so also now, Christ shall be conspicuously and gloriously
manifested, whether through life or through death, for, so far as
I am concerned, to be living, both as to my very existence and
my experience, that is Christ, and to have died, is gain.

But if for me life in the flesh be my portion, this very thing
(namely, life in the flesh) is that in which the fruit of my ministry will be involved, and is the condition of that fruit being
brought forth. Then, what I shall prefer for myself, I do not

*make known. Rather, I am being held motionless by an equal pull from the two (namely, life and death), so that I cannot incline either way, having the passionate desire towards striking my tent and being with Christ, which is by far better, but still to remain with my flesh is more needful for your sakes. And having come to this settled conviction (namely, that to remain in the flesh is more needful for you), I know that I shall remain and continue alive with you all for your progress and joy in your faith, in order that your rejoicing may abound in Christ Jesus through me by reason of my personal presence with you again.*

*Only (since my only reason for remaining on earth is for your progress in the Christian life), see to it that you recognize your responsibility as citizens (of heaven), and put yourselves to the absolute necessity of performing the duties devolving upon you in that position, doing this in a manner which is befitting to the gospel of Christ, in order that whether having come and having seen you, or whether being absent, I am hearing the things concerning you, namely, that you are standing firm in one spirit, holding your ground, with one soul contending (as a team of athletes would) in perfect cooperation with one another for the faith of the gospel, and not being affrighted in even one thing by those who are entrenched in their opposition against you, which failure on your part to be frightened is an indication of such a nature as to present clear evidence to them of utter destruction, also clear evidence of your salvation, and this evidence from God. And the reason why you should not be terrified is because to you that very thing was graciously given for the sake of Christ and in His behalf, not only to be believing on Him, but also to be suffering for His sake and in His behalf, having the same struggle which you saw in me and now hear to be in me.*

*In view of the fact that there is a certain ground of appeal in Christ which exhorts, since there is a certain tender persuasion that comes from divine love, in view of the fact that there is a certain joint-participation with the Spirit in a common interest*

*and activity, since there are certain tenderheartednesses and com-
passionate yearnings and actions, fill full my joy by thinking the
same thing, having the same love, being in heart agreement,
thinking the one thing, doing nothing impelled by a spirit of
factiousness, nothing impelled by empty pride, but in lowliness
of mind consider one another as excelling themselves, this estimation resting, not upon feelings or sentiment, but upon a due
consideration of facts, not consulting each one his own interests
only, but also each one the interests of others.*

*This mind be constantly having in you which was also in
Christ Jesus, who has always been and at present continues to
subsist in that mode of being in which He gives outward expression of His essential nature, that of Deity, and who did not after
weighing the facts, consider it a treasure to be clutched and
retained at all hazards, to be equal with Deity (in the expression
of the divine essence), but emptied Himself, having taken the
outward expression of a bondslave, which expression came from
and was truly representative of His nature, entering into a new
state of existence, that of mankind. And being found to be in
outward guise as man, He stooped very low, having become obedient to the extent of death, even such a death as that upon a
cross.*

*Because of which voluntary act of supreme self-renunciation,
God also super-eminently exalted Him to the highest rank and
power, and graciously bestowed upon Him THE NAME, the one
which is above every name, in order that in recognition of THE
NAME belonging to Jesus, every knee should bow, of things in
heaven, of things on earth, and of things under the earth, and in
order that every tongue should plainly and openly declare that
Jesus Christ is LORD, resulting in the glory of God the Father.*

*Wherefore, my beloved ones, as you have always obeyed, not
as in my presence only, but much more in my absence, carry to
its ultimate conclusion your own salvation with fear and trembling, for God is the One who is constantly putting forth His
power in you, both in the form of the constant activity of (your)*

*being desirous of and the constant activity of (your) putting into operation His good pleasure. All things be constantly doing without discontented and secret mutterings and grumblings, and without discussions which carry an undertone of suspicion or doubt, to the end that you may become those who are deserving of no censure, free from fault or defect, and guileless in their simplicity, children of God without blemish, in the midst of a perverse and distorted generation, among whom you appear as luminaries in the world, holding forth the Word of life, to the end that I may have a ground for glorying reserved for the day of Christ, this glorying being because of the fact that I have not run in vain nor have I labored to the point of exhaustion in vain. In fact, if also I am being poured out as a libation upon the altar and priestly service of your faith, I rejoice and continue to rejoice with you all. But as for you, you even be rejoicing in the same thing and continue to rejoice with me.*

*But I am hoping in the Lord quickly to send Timothy to you, in order that I also may be of good cheer, having come to know of your circumstances. For not even one do I have who is like-souled, one of such a character who would genuinely and with no secondary regard for himself be concerned about the welfare of your circumstances. For one and all without exception are constantly seeking their own things, not the things of Christ Jesus. But you know by experience his character which has been approved after having been tested, that as a child to a father, with me he has served in the furtherance of the gospel. Him therefore I am hoping to send as soon as, having turned my attention from other things and having concentrated it upon my own situation, I shall have ascertained my position. But I have come to a settled conviction, which conviction is in the Lord, that I also myself shall come shortly.*

*But after weighing the facts, I considered it indispensable to send to you Epaphroditus, my brother and fellow-worker and fellow-soldier, but your ambassador to whom you entrusted a mission, and he who in a sacred way ministered to my needs, for he was constantly yearning after you, and was in sore anguish because you heard that he was sick; for truly he was ill, next door to death. But God had mercy upon him, and not upon him alone, but also on me, in order that I might not have sorrow upon sorrow. With increased haste and diligence therefore I sent him, in order that having seen him again, you may recover your cheerfulness and my sorrow may be lessened. Receive him to yourselves therefore with all joy, and hold such ones in honor, value them highly, and deem them precious, because on account of the work of Christ he drew near to death, having recklessly exposed his life in order that he might supply that which was lacking in your service to me.*

*As for the rest (of which I wish to say to you), go on constantly rejoicing in the Lord. To go on writing the same things to you is not to me irksome or tedious, while for you it is safe. Keep a watchful eye ever upon the dogs. Keep a watchful eye ever upon the evil workers. Keep a watchful eye ever upon those who are mutilated, doing this for the purpose of bewaring of and avoiding the same. For, as for us, we are the circumcision, those who by the Spirit of God are rendering service and obedience, and who are exulting in Christ Jesus, and who have not come to a settled persuasion, trusting in the flesh. Although as for myself, I might be having confidence even in the flesh.*

*If (as is the case) anyone else presumes to have come to a settled persuasion, trusting in the flesh, I could occupy that place, and with more reason; eight days old in circumcision, my origin, from Israelitish stock, belonging to the tribe of Benjamin, a Hebrew from true Hebrew parents, with reference to the law, a Pharisee, with regard to zeal, a persecutor of the Church, with reference to that kind of righteousness which is in the law, become blameless. But the things which were of such a nature as to be gains to me, these things I have set down for the sake of Christ as a loss. Yea, indeed, therefore, at least, even, I am still setting all things down to be a loss for the sake of that which excels all others, my knowledge of Christ Jesus my Lord which*

*I have gained through experience, for which sake I have been caused to forfeit all things, and I am still counting them dung, in order that Christ I might gain, yea, in order that I might through observation of others be discovered by them to be in Christ, not having as my righteousness that righteousness which is of the law, but that righteousness which is from God on the basis of faith.*

*Yes, for His sake I have been caused to forfeit all things, and I count them but dung, in order that I might come to know Him in an experiential way, and to come to know experientially the power of His resurrection, and a joint-participation in His sufferings, being brought to the place where my life will radiate a likeness to His death, if by any means I might arrive at my goal, namely, the out-resurrection out from among those who are dead. Not that I have already made acquisition or that I have now already been brought to that place of settled spiritual maturity beyond which there is no progress, but I am pursuing onward if I may lay hold on that for which I have been laid hold of by Christ Jesus.*

*Brethren, as for myself, as I look back upon my life and calmly draw a conclusion, I am not counting myself yet as one who has in an absolute and complete way laid hold (of that for which I have been laid hold of by Christ Jesus); but one thing, I, in fact am forgetting completely the things that are behind, but am stretching forward to the things that are in front; bearing down upon the goal, I am pursuing on for the prize of the call from above of God which is in Christ Jesus.*

*As many therefore as are spiritually mature, let us be of this mind. And, if (as is the case), in anything you are differently minded, and that, in an evil sense, this also will God reveal to you. Only one thing, so far as we have come, let us keep our lives in the same path. Become imitators of me, brethren, and observe attentively those who conduct themselves in a manner which reflects the example which you have in us, for many are going about, concerning whom I often have been telling you,*

*but now tell you weeping, enemies (they are) of the cross of
Christ, whose end is utter destruction, whose god is their belly
and that which they esteem to be their glory is their shame, who
regard the things upon the earth. For the commonwealth of
which we are citizens, has its fixed location in heaven, out from
which we with our attention withdrawn from all else, are eagerly
waiting to welcome the Saviour, the Lord Jesus Christ, and to
receive Him to ourselves: who will transform our humiliated body,
conforming it to the body of His glory, by means of the energy
through which He is able to marshal all things under Himself.*

*Therefore, my brothers, individually loved ones, and individ-
ually passionately longed for, my joy and my victor's festal
garland, thus be standing firm in the Lord, beloved ones. Euodia
I exhort, please, and Syntyche, I exhort, please, to be of the
same mind in the Lord. Even so, I make request of you also,
Syzygus, who art a genuine yokefellow in deed as well as in
name, lend a hand with these women in their efforts to settling
the differences which they have between themselves, women of
such a character that in the gospel they labored and contended
in perfect cooperation with me (as a team of athletes would),
together also with Clement and the rest of my fellow-workers
whose names are in the book of life. Be rejoicing in the Lord
always. Again I say, be rejoicing. Let your sweet reasonableness, your forbearance, your being satisfied with less than your
due, become known to all men. The Lord is near. Stop perpetually worrying about even one thing, but in everything, by
prayer whose essence is that of worship and devotion, and by
supplication which is a cry for your personal needs, let your
requests with thanksgiving for the things asked for be made
known in the presence of God, and the peace of God which surpasses all power of comprehension, shall mount guard over your
hearts and minds in Christ Jesus.*

*Finally, brethren, whatever things have the character of truth,
whatever things are worthy of reverence, whatever things are
righteous, whatever things are pure, whatever things are lovely,*

*whatever things are attractive, whatever excellence there may be or fit object of praise, these things make the subject of careful reflection. The things also which you learned and received and heard and saw in me, these things, habitually practice: and the God of peace shall be with you.*

*But I rejoiced in the Lord greatly that already once more you let your care for me blossom into activity again, in which matter you were all along thoughtful, but you never had an opportunity. It is not that I speak as regards want, for, so far as I am concerned, I have come to learn, in the circumstances in which I am placed, to be independent of these and self-sufficient. I know in fact how to keep myself low; I know in fact how to have more than enough. In everything and in all things I have learned the secret, both to be satiated and to be hungry, and to have more than enough and to lack. I am strong for all things in the One who constantly infuses strength in me.*

*All the same, you did a beautiful thing when you made yourselves fellow-partakers with my tribulation. But, you yourselves also know, Philippians, that at the beginning of the gospel, when I went out from Macedonia, not even one assembly made itself a partner with me as regards an account of giving and taking except only you, that even in Thessalonica more than once you sent to relieve my necessities. Not that it is my character to be ever seeking the gift, but I am seeking the fruit which is accumulating to your account. But I have all things to the full and overflowing. I have been filled completely full and at present am well supplied, having received at the hand of Epaphroditus the things from you, a scent of sweet savor, a sacrifice acceptable, well-pleasing to God. But my God shall satisfy to the full all your need in accordance with His wealth in glory in Christ Jesus.*

*Now to God even our Father, be the glory for ever and ever. Amen. Greet every saint in Christ Jesus. The brethren with me send greeting. All the saints send greeting, especially those of Caesar's household. The grace of the Lord Jesus Christ be with your spirit, with all of you and in this respect individually.*

# THE OUTLINE OF PAUL'S LETTER

# 1.

## PAUL GREETS THE SAINTS AT PHILIPPI (1:1, 2)

### Verse one

THE writer of this letter to the Philippians had two names, Saul, which means "to ask or pray," his Hebrew name, and Paul, coming from the Latin, meaning "little," his Gentile name. Some think that he had the two names in childhood. The practice of adopting Gentile names may be traced through all the periods of Hebrew history. When Paul became the apostle to the Gentiles, he discarded his Hebrew name (Acts 13:9). There are indications that Paul was small in stature, hence his Latin name. He was a man of prayer, and thus lived up to his Hebrew name.

Paul's practice of beginning his letters with the name of the writer, followed by the name of the recipient, which in turn was followed by a greeting ("Paul . . . to all the saints in Christ Jesus which are at Philippi, with the bishops and deacons, grace be unto you and peace, from God our Father and from the Lord Jesus Christ"), is not peculiar to the Bible epistles. Paul simply followed the custom of the day. Pliny the younger, writing to the Emperor Trajan, begins his letter, "Pliny, to the emperor Trajan, wisheth health. It is my custom, Sir, etc." The emperor answers, "Trajan to Pliny, health and happiness. You have taken the right method, my Pliny, etc." Adolph Deissman, in his monumental work on the Greek papyri, *Light from the Ancient East,* gives instances of the same custom. A letter from an Egyptian to a family in mourning, second century A.D., begins as follows: "Irene to Taonnophris and Philo, good comfort. I am so sorry and weep over the departed one as I wept for Didymas." A letter of an Egyptian soldier to his father, second century A.D., begins: "Apion to Epimachus his father and lord, many greetings. Before all things I pray that thou art in health, and that thou dost prosper and fare well continually." Is not this just like John's letter, "The elder unto the well-beloved Gaius, whom I love in the truth. Beloved, I wish above all things that thou mayest prosper and be in health, even as thy soul prospereth" (III John 1, 2)? Then there is a letter from a prodigal son to his mother: "Antonis Longus to Nilus his mother, many greetings. And continually do I pray that thou art in health."

The name "Timothy" is a combination of two Greek words which together mean, "he who honors God." The Greek word for "honor" has in it the ideas of reverence and veneration. Possibly, his grandmother Lois was responsible for the naming of the child, and also for much of the religious training he received, so that when Timothy grew to manhood, he exhibited those qualities in his life. These were the qualities which perhaps attracted Paul to the young man.

Paul calls Timothy and himself servants of Jesus Christ. There is no definite article in the Greek. They were servants by nature. The word is *doulos*,[1] and refers to one bound to another. Paul was bound to Jesus Christ by the bands of a constraining love. It refers to one born into slavery. Paul was born into slavery to sin by his first birth, and into the position of a loving bondslave of the Lord Jesus by his new birth. It refers to one who is in a relation to another which only death can break. Paul's relation to Satan was broken by his identification with Christ in His death. He now is in a relation to Jesus Christ which will last forever, since Christ can never die again, and Paul's life is Christ. It refers to one whose will is swallowed up in the will of another. Paul's will was at one time swallowed up in the will of Satan.

---

1. *Nuggets*, pp. 45, 46.

Now his will is swallowed up in the sweet will of God. It refers to one who serves another even to the disregard of his own interests. Paul served Satan to the detriment of his own interests. Now he serves the Lord Jesus with a reckless abandon, not regarding his own interests.

The name "Christ" is the English spelling of the Greek word *Christos*, which in turn is the translation of the Hebrew word meaning "Messiah." The word "Christ" means "The Anointed One." The name "Jesus" is the English spelling of the Greek *Iesous*, which is in turn the Greek spelling of the Hebrew word *Jehoshua* which means "Jehovah saves." We have therefore in these two names, the Messianic office of our Lord, His deity, and His substitutionary atonement.

Paul is writing to the saints. The word "saint"[1] is the translation of a Greek word meaning "to set apart," in its verb, and "set apart ones," in its noun form. The pagan Greeks set apart buildings as temples, consecrating them for non-secular, and therefore, religious purposes. These became the objects of veneration and reverence. Thus, saints are believing sinners set apart from sin to holiness, set apart from Satan to God, thus being consecrated for Gods' sacred fellowship and service. The word "saint" as a designation of a Christian, brings at once to our attention the duty of every believer, that of living a separated life. The words, "saint, sanctify, holy," are all translations of this same Greek root. They all speak of the absolute separation from evil and dedication to God, that must always be true of the Christian believer.

Paul uses the word "all" because he wishes to put those Philippians who had not sent to his support, on a level with those who had. There were some divisions among the Philippians, and Paul set himself above these.

---

1. *Treasures*, pp. 67-70.

The phrase "in Christ Jesus" was necessary in defining just who these saints were. The Greek word "saint" was used in Philippi as a name for individual worshippers in the pagan Greek religions. Paul wished to differentiate the saints of God from the "saints" in the Greek mystery religions. The word "in" is used with the locative of sphere. These saints were saints in the sphere of Christ. That is, Christ is the sphere in which the believer has his new life and all his interests and activities. The believer's new existence is circumscribed by Christ. Paul put this in other words in the expression, "For to me to live is Christ." That is, the new life Paul has is Christ, which issues in a Christ-like life. Here again we have separation, for that which surrounds the believer, namely, Christ in whom he is ensphered, separates him from all else.

The word "bishop" is the translation of a Greek word used in secular pursuits, of an overseer in any capacity, for instance, the official in charge of the repairing of a temple or an officer in an army. The word itself means "to look upon." Paul uses it as another name for an elder, the latter being the title of the office so far as status in the church is concerned, the former being the title that indicated the responsibility and activity of the office, that of overseeing the spiritual welfare of the local church. He brings the two names together as designating one individual in Acts 20:17, 28.

The word "deacon" is the English spelling of a Greek word that was used as a general term to designate a servant. It covered both slaves and hired servants. It represented a servant, not in his relation to his master, but in his activity. The same word is translated "minister" in I Corinthians 3:5; II Corinthians 3:6; Ephesians 3:7. Here it refers to a distinct class of officers in the apostolic church. The origin of the office is given us in Acts 6: The care of the sick and the poor however led to spiritual ministrations. Stephen and Philip are examples of those early church deacons who ministered in the Word. Translation: *Paul and Timothy, bondslaves by nature, belonging to Christ Jesus, to all the consecrated and separated ones in Christ Jesus, together with the overseers and ministering deacons.*

### Verse two

The Greek word for "grace" is a wonderful word. Archbishop Trench says of it, *It is hardly too much to say that the Greek mind has in no word uttered itself and all that was at its heart more distinctly than in this.* When this word is brought over into the New Testament one can repeat Trench's statement, substituting the word "God" for "Greek." *It is hardly too much to say that God has in no word uttered Himself and all that is in His heart more distinctly than in this.* In its use among the pagan Greeks it referred to a favor done by one Greek to another out of the pure generosity of his heart, and with no hope of reward. When it is used in the New Testament, it refers to that favor which God did at Calvary when He stepped down from His judgment throne to take upon Himself the guilt and penalty of human sin. In the case of the Greek, the favor was done to a friend, never an enemy. In the case of God it was an enemy, the sinner, bitter in his hatred of God, for whom the favor was done. God has no strings tied to the salvation He procured for man at the Cross. Salvation is given the believing sinner out of the pure generosity of God's heart. The Greek word referred to an action that was beyond the ordinary course of what might be expected, and was therefore commendable. What a description of that which took place at the Cross! The grace spoken of here is sanctifying grace, that part of salvation given the saint in which God causes him to grow in Christlikeness through the ministry of the Holy Spirit.

The word "peace" in classical Greek means "to bind together," in the New Testament, "the operation of God's grace in binding the believing sinner to God and His life again, this operation con-

tinued in bringing that believer in his experience more and more
into harmony with God in his life and service," the latter being the
particular phase to which Paul refers here. Translation: (*Sancti-*
*fying*) *grace be to you, and* (*heart*) *peace, from God our Father*
*and from the Lord Jesus Christ.*

## 2

## PAUL THANKS GOD FOR THE CO-OPERATION OF THE PHILIPPIAN SAINTS IN THE WORK OF THE GOSPEL, AND PRAYS FOR THEM (1:3-11)

### Verses three and four

The word "upon" does not mean "at." That is, Paul does not mean here that he thanks God at every remembrance of the Philippians. It means "upon the basis of." That is, the Philippians form the basis for Paul's thanksgiving. The word "every" in the Greek text has the idea of "whole." Paul thanks God because of his whole remembrance of the Philippians. There were no regrets in all of Paul's relationships with them. Translation: *I am thanking my God constantly for my whole remembrance of you, always in every prayer of mine making supplication for you all with joy.*

### Verse five

The word "fellowship" in the original means, "a joint-participation in a common interest and activity." This was the meaning of the word "fellowship" when the Authorized Version was made. The English word has largely lost its original meaning in religious circles, although it has retained it in academic phraseology. The word "fellowship" today usually means "companionship, intercourse between individuals." This was the Philippian's joint-participation with Paul in a common interest and activity, that of preaching the gospel. The preposition "in" is a preposition of motion. This common interest and activity was in the progress of

the gospel. The Philippians supported Paul with their prayers
and finances while he went about his missionary labors. This is
what he is thanking God for. And this is part of that "whole remembrance" of them for which he is grateful. This joint-participation in the work of propagating the gospel had gone on from
the first day when Lydia had opened her home to the preaching
of the Word (Acts 16:15), until the moment when Paul was writing this letter. Paul was grateful to God for all their help. And
he was thanking them also. There is a most delicate touch here
that cannot be brought out in any English translation, since the
English language does not have the idiom. In the Greek there is a
definite article before the adverb "now." That is, Paul was thanking God for the joint-participation of the Philippians with him in
the great missionary enterprise from the first day until *the* now.
The article "the" is a delicate Pauline finger pointing to the gift
which the Philippians had just sent with Epaphroditus, their messenger. Paul thanks them in so many words at the end of his letter. But here he does not want to appear too hastily and obtrusively
grateful. So he thanks God for all of their help, and points a
delicate finger consisting of the Greek definite article, used before
an adverb, at the most recent gift as included in the "whole remembrance." Translation: *I am constantly thanking my God for
your joint-participation in the furtherance of the gospel from the
first day until this particular moment.*

## Verse six

The words "being confident," have a slight causitive force in
the Greek. Coupled with his thanksgiving for their past generous
aid in the cause of foreign missions, is his thanksgiving for their
future aid, since he is confident of their future help. The word
translated "confident," speaks of the fact that Paul had come to a
settled persuasion concerning the fact that the God who had begun
in the Philippians the good work of giving to missions, would
bring it to a successful conclusion right up to the day of Christ

Jesus. The word translated "until," assumes the nearness of the Rapture in Paul's mind and outlook. Translation: *Having come to this settled and firm persuasion concerning this very thing, that He who began in you a work which is good, will bring it to a successful conclusion right up to the day of Christ Jesus;*

### Verse seven

The word translated "meet" has the idea of "right" or "just." That is, Paul says that it is no more than right or just on his part to think this of them, namely, their continued joint-participation with him in missionary work. The word translated "think," speaks of the action of a person constantly having his mind directed in a practical way in the good interest of someone. Paul's mind, turned in the direction of the Philippians, would soon turn to prayer in their behalf. The expression "because I have you in my heart," could just as properly be, "because you have me in your heart." The second way of rendering the Greek is more in accord with the context. The Philippians had a large place in their hearts for Paul, and at this time especially with reference to the two particulars mentioned here, first, with reference to his defense of the gospel, and second, in his confirmation of the same.

The word "defense" is a Greek judicial term referring to an attorney talking his client off from a charge, thus presenting a verbal defense. Paul was defending the Faith before the tribunal of the world, Nero's throne. A successful defense would result in the gospel being confirmed, that is, made stable in the sense that its claims would be shown to be true. In this joint-participation of the Philippians, not only in the missionary enterprise but in the defense and establishment of the gospel, Paul says that they were partakers of his grace. The word "my" is to be connected with "partakers," not "grace." The Philippians were Paul's co-sharers in the grace of God. Their love and kindness to him in his dark moments, constituted proof of the fact that they were joint-participants with Paul in the grace that resulted in their joint efforts at propagating the gospel. Translation: *Even as it is right for me to be constantly turning my mind in the direction of this very thing in your behalf (namely, the completion of God's good work in you), because you are holding me in your heart both in my bonds and in my defense and confirmation of the gospel, you all being co-sharers with me in this grace.*

## Verse eight

The word "record" is the translation of the Greek word meaning "one who bears testimony." It is the word from which we get "martyr." Such adjuration of God, Paul uses only in solemn personal statements. The words "long after" are in the Greek, a verb meaning "to desire earnestly, to have a strong affection for." The prefixed preposition is intensive in its use, intensifying the meaning of the verb. But one can also see a local usage. Not only does Paul have an intense desire or longing for the Philippians, but he longs over them. What a miracle of divine grace for this heretofore proud Pharisee to have tender heart-longings for these former pagan Greeks! But that is not all. He tells them that this longing is in the bowels of Jesus Christ. The inner organs, here designated by the word "bowels," were regarded by the ancients as the seat of the tender affections. The word used here refers to the upper organs, the stomach, liver, and lungs, another word being used for the intestines. We would say "the heart." Paul thus describes his longing, not as his individual emotion, but as Christ's longing, as if the very heart of Christ dwelt in Paul. The great apostle lived so close to the Lord Jesus, and he had so shared the sufferings of his Lord for righteousness' sake, that his heart was very tender, and beat as one with the heart of Jesus. Translation: *For my witness is God, how I long after all of you with the tenderheartedness of Christ Jesus.*

## Verse nine

"Pray" is the translation of a word which speaks of prayer directed consciously to God, and with a definite aim. As Paul prayed, he had a definite consciousness of the presence of God, and that he was speaking, not into mere space, but to a Person, and that that Person was listening, giving attention to what he was saying. The word "that" could also be rendered, "this is the purport and substance of my prayer."

The love spoken of here is the love that God is (I John 4:16), produced in the heart of the yielded believer by the Holy Spirit (Rom. 5:5), its chief ingredient, self-sacrifice for the benefit of the one who is loved (John 3:16), and its constituent elements analyzed for us in I Corinthians 13: "Abound" is from a Greek word which means "to exceed a fixed number or measure, to exist in superfluity." This divine love, an exotic flower from heaven, planted in the foreign soil of the believer's heart (I John 3:1, "what manner of," namely, "what foreign kind of"), was existing in superabundance in the hearts of these Greeks who had been saved out of gross paganism, and was overflowing into the hearts of others. Paul prays that it might increase.

But like a river in flood-time, its volume needed to be brought within guiding limitations lest it work harm rather than bring blessing. There was an eager and enthusiastic spirit among these new converts, but a lack of a deep understanding of the truth, and also a lack of a sensitive moral perception and tact. So Paul prays that this love may overflow more and more, but that its outflow and application might be brought within the guiding limitations of knowledge and judgment. "Knowledge" is from the Greek work speaking of knowledge gained by experience, as contrasted to intuitive knowledge, which is from another word. A prefixed preposition intensifies the word, and we have "full knowledge." The full knowledge which these Philippians needed to gain by experience was a better understanding of God's Word as translated into their experience, and a clearer vision of the Lord Jesus in all the beauty and fragrance of His Person. A Christian can have an "understanding" knowledge of the Word, that is, be able to explain its meaning to others, without having an experiential knowledge of the same. But when that Christian has put the Word of God into practice in his life, then he has what Paul is talking about here. This is the difference between a young convert and a matured believer. The former has not had time to live long enough to live out the Word in his life, the latter has. The former, if his life is wholly yielded, is a delight to look upon in his Christian life, as one would enjoy the vigor and sparkle of youth. The latter, in his mellowed, well-rounded, matured, and fully-developed Christian experience, his life full of tender reminiscences of his years of companionship with the Lord Jesus, has the fragrance of heavenly things about him. This was what the Philippian saints needed, but it would take time for this to be brought about. This mellowed Christian experience would constitute the limitations thrown around this overflowing love that would insure its proper application and wise outreach.

The words "all judgment" are the translation of a Greek word referring to a sensitive moral perception, and a quickness of ethical tact. How often we saints mean to be loving to others, and say the wrong words or do the wrong thing. We lack that delicate sensibility, that ability to express ourselves correctly, that gentle, wise, discriminating touch which would convey the love we have in our hearts to the lives of others. But this can be ours if we but live in close companionship with the One who always exhibited that sense of delicate tactfulness in His life. Translation: *And this is the constant purport of my definite petitions, namely, that your love yet more and more may overflow, but at the same time be kept within the guiding limitations of an accurate knowledge gained by experience and those of every kind of sensitive moral and ethical tact.*

## Verses ten and eleven

Paul prays that the love manifested by the saints might be guided into proper channels by the limiting factors of a full and experiential knowledge and a sensitive moral and ethical tact, in order that they may be able to approve things that are excellent. The word "approve"[1] is from a Greek word which refers to the act of testing something for the purpose of approving it, thus "to approve after testing." It was used of the standing of candidates for the degree of doctor of medicine, who had passed their examinations. They were certified physicians. Here the word refers to the ability of the saints to sift or test a certain thing and thus to recognize its worth and put their stamp of approval upon it. The expression "the things that are more excellent" (the definite article is used in the Greek, pointing to particular things), comes from a word that means "to carry two ways," thus "to carry different ways," thus "to differ." It refers here to those moral and spiritual concepts and actions which involve delicate and keen distinctions, those that require a deep and keen discernment to recognize. Not the ordinary, every-day, easily-understood spiritual obligations, but the finer points of Christian conduct are in the apostle's mind. The Greek word is found in an early secular document in the sentence, "you are *superior* to Ptolemais in experience," and in the phrase *"most vital* interests in the treasury." It speaks of those things therefore that are superior, vital, that surpass, that excel. Thus, a Spirit-produced love in the heart and life of the saint, which has been confined like a river within the limiting banks of a full experiential knowledge and a sensitive moral and ethical tact, is the thing that sharpens the moral and spiritual perceptions for the discernment of the finer qualities of Christian conduct. This will result in the saint being sincere and without offence until the day of Christ, which latter expression refers to the Rapture of the Church.

"Sincere" is from a Greek word which means "distinct, unmixed, pure, unsullied." There is no hypocrisy about such a saint. His life is open like a book waiting to be read. "Without offence" is literally, "not cut against, not stumbled against." This saint is not a stumbling block to others. Translation: *So that you may*

---

1. *Treasures,* pp. 126-131.

*after testing, recognize the true value of the finer points of Chris-*
*tian conduct and thus sanction them, in order that you may be*
*pure and not a stumbling block, keeping in view the day of*
*Christ, being filled full with the fruit of righteousness, which fruit*
*is through Jesus Christ, resulting in glory and praise to God.*

## 3.

## PAUL ASSURES THE SAINTS THAT HIS CIRCUMSTANCES HAVE BROUGHT ABOUT A PIONEER ADVANCE OF THE GOSPEL (1:12-26).

### Verse twelve

EPAPHRODITUS had told Paul that the Church at Philippi was afraid that his imprisonment was curtailing his missionary work. Paul assures them that the contrary has been the case. The gospel has made pioneer advances by reason of his circumscribed activities. The word "would" speaks of a desire that has purpose and intention back of it. It is "will" with determination. The desire came after mature consideration. "Understand" is from the word meaning "to acquire knowledge by experience." The Philippian saints, he desired, should learn something from his experience. "The things which happened unto me," are literally, "the things dominating me." The words "which happened" are not in the Greek text and are not needed. Nothing ever just happens to the saint. Things either come directly from God or they reach us from some other source by His permissive will. The things that were then dominating Paul's life were those connected with his imprisonment. "Have fallen out" is literally, "have come to result." The use of "rather" tells us that the Philippians were thinking that Paul's ministry was being curtailed. The word "furtherance" is from a Greek word which means "to cut before," and is thought to have been used of an army of pioneer wood cutters which precedes the regular army, cutting a road through an impenetrable forest, thus making possible the pioneer advance of the latter into regions where otherwise it could not have gone. Paul assures the Philippian saints that his circumstances have not only failed to curtail his missionary work, but they have advanced it, and not only that, they have brought about a pioneer advance in regions where otherwise it could not have gone. It is so in our lives. Our God-ordained or God-permitted circumstances are used of God to provide for a pioneer advance of the gospel in our Christian service. Translation: *But after mature consideration I desire you to gain this knowledge from (my) experience, that my circumstances have come to result rather in the pioneer advance of the gospel.*

### Verse thirteen

The word "bonds" refers to Paul being a prisoner of the Roman empire. "Manifest" is the translation of a Greek word meaning, "to make known what has been unknown, to become known, to be plainly recognized, thoroughly understood." "Are" is from a word meaning "to become." The phrase "in Christ," is to be construed with "are manifest," not "bonds." The question of the reason for Paul's imprisonment was raised, and the word was passed around that it was because of his relationship to Christ. The next question would be, "Who is Christ?" And the gospel story would be told. It became known and understood that Paul was in prison because he preached the gospel.

The word "palace" refers in the Greek to the Praetorian Guard, composed of the soldiers of the imperial regiments whose barracks were at Rome. Paul had been living in his own rented quarters near these barracks, guarded by soldiers twenty-four hours a day. He lived for two years with a Roman soldier chained to his wrist. As the different soldiers would take their turn guarding Paul, they would hear the conversations he had with his visitors, conversations full of the gospel and of the Saviour of sinners.

They would hear the apostle pray, and would listen as he dictated the epistles he wrote. The noble prisoner would talk to them about their souls, talking in the international Greek so common in those days. Thus, the gospel went through the barracks of the Roman soldiers, a place where it would not have gone, if Paul had not been a prisoner there. Translation: *So that it has become plainly recognized that my bonds are because of Christ, throughout the whole Praetorian Guard and to all the rest.*

### Verse fourteen

In addition to the gospel making a pioneer advance throughout the Praetorian Guard, Paul speaks of the increase of preaching in the city of Rome itself. The word "many" is literally, "the most." Most of the Christian brethren were preaching now, the implication being that a few held back. Persecutions in Rome had somewhat silenced gospel preaching there. The words "waxing confident" come from a word which means "to persuade." These Christians had been persuaded by the brave and fearless example of Paul in prison, and had come to a state of settled confidence in the Lord. The words, "in the Lord" are to be construed with "waxing confident," not "brethren." They became more abundantly bold to speak the Word. The boldness required to profess Christ in Rome is illustrated by a wall scribble. A caricature of Christ on the Cross with an ass' head is portrayed, while on the left appears a Christian youth in an attitude of adoration. Underneath are the words, "Alexamenos worships God." The word "speak" denotes the fact, not the substance of the speaking. They had broken silence. Translation: *And the great majority of the brethren having come to a state of settled confidence in the Lord by reason of the fact that they have been persuaded by my bonds, are more abundantly bold, fearlessly breaking their silence and speaking the Word.*

### Verses fifteen to seventeen

After telling the Philippians that one result of his imprisonment was to increase the number of gospel witnesses, he speaks of
the two groups into which they were divided, and the different
motives that impelled them to break their silence, which motives
were governed by their different attitudes toward Paul. The preposition "of" in verse fifteen is the translation of a Greek word
meaning "because of." One group preached because it was en-
vious of Paul and was at odds with him. This group was composed of the Judaizers, Jews who taught that the Gentiles had to
enter Christianity through the gate of Judaism. They preached
Christ, but their real object was to gain adherents to the law.
They valued success, not as a triumph over paganism, but as a
triumph over Paul. It would make them feel good if they could
make his sufferings in prison more acute by reason of jealousy
which might arise in his heart.

The other group was composed of Gentile converts, friends of
Paul, who were encouraged to preach by the thought that it
would give joy to the great apostle whose liberty was restricted.
The word "contention" is the translation of a Greek word speaking of self-seeking partisanship, intrigue, a factious, selfish spirit.
"Defense" is from a technical word in the law courts speaking of
the verbal defense presented by a lawyer who defends his client.
The word "set" is literally "appointed." Translation: *In fact,
certain ones even because of envy and rivalry, but also others because of good will are proclaiming Christ; some indeed out of a
spirit of love, knowing that I am appointed for the defense of the
gospel; but others out of a partisan self-seeking spirit are announcing Christ, not with pure unmixed motives, but insincerely,
thinking to make my chain gall me.*

### Verse eighteen

But observe the effect all this had on the great apostle. The
Greek for "what then" could be rendered, "What is my feeling

thereupon?" "Every way" has the idea of "in every way or manner" of preaching method. "Pretext" is from a Greek word
which has in it the idea of an ulterior motive. Paul rejoices that
the people get some knowledge of Christ. Translation: *What is
my feeling in view of these things? (Supposing they do purpose
to make my chain gall me). The only thing that follows is that
in every manner whether in pretense or in truth, whether insincerely or sincerely, Christ is being announced; and in this I am
rejoicing, and certainly I will continue to rejoice.*

### Verses nineteen and twenty

The word "this" refers to the fact that Christ is being more
widely announced as a result of Paul's imprisonment. The Greek
word "salvation" is used in the New Testament to refer not only
to the spiritual salvation of the individual, but also to the healing
of the body (Matt. 9:21, 22), and of self-preservation in a physical
sense, or of the well-being of the individual (Mark 15:30, 31).
Paul uses it here of his own well-being. The knowledge that his
imprisonment was not hindering the preaching of the gospel, but
on the other hand was cutting pioneer roads for its advance, and
causing many in Rome to break their silence and proclaim the
Word, was like a tonic to his soul, saving him from discourage-
ment and spurring him on to greater endeavor in his service for
his Lord. But even these encouraging facts would not in themselves have been enough to produce that result unless the Philippians would pray for his spiritual welfare, and the Holy Spirit
would in answer to their prayers minister to Paul's spiritual needs
in the midst of these circumstances.

This salvation of which Paul speaks, is described as to its nature in verse twenty. The words "earnest expectation" are from
a Greek word made up of three words, "away, the head, to watch."
It describes a person with head erect and outstretched, whose
attention is turned away from all other objects and riveted upon
just one. The word is used in the Greek classics of the watchman

who peered into the darkness, eagerly looking for the first gleam
of the distant beacon which would announce the capture of Troy.
It is that concentrated, intense hope which ignores other interests
and strains forward as with outstretched head, that was Paul's
attitude of heart. The Greek word translated "boldness" gives us
the key to the understanding of the sentence, "in nothing I shall
be ashamed." It means literally "all speech," thus, "freedom of
speech." In Paul's difficult position, a prisoner of the Roman
empire, there was a danger of failure on his part to maintain
that bold and fearless testimony which was his habit all through
his missionary career. This testimony had to do here not only
with his spoken words but also with his life. It was the intense
desire of his heart that Christ be magnified in him, whether by a
life lived in the fullness of the Spirit or in a martyr's death. The
word "magnify" is the translation of a Greek word meaning, "to
make great, to make conspicuous, to get glory and praise." Paul's
desire was that the Lord Jesus might be seen in his life in all His
beauty, that He might be conspicuous, that He might get glory and
praise to Himself through Paul. Translation: *For I know that
this for me shall result in salvation through your petition and
through the bountiful supply of the Spirit of Jesus Christ. And
this is exactly in accordance with my undivided and intense expectancy and hope, namely, that in respect to not even one thing
shall I be ashamed, but in every boldness of speech as always so
now, Christ shall be conspicuously and gloriously manifested,
whether through life or through death.*

## Verse twenty-one

Paul is determined that Christ shall be radiated through his
life, and so he says, "For to me to live is Christ." His words in
Colossians 3:4, "Christ, our life," help us to understand this
statement. Christ is Paul's life in that He is that eternal life which
Paul received in salvation, a life which is ethical in its content,
and which operates in Paul as a motivating, energizing, pulsating

principle of existence that transforms Paul's life, a divine Person living His life in and through the apostle. All of Paul's activities, all of his interests, the entire round of his existence is ensphered within that circumference which is Christ. The words, "to die" are more accurately, "to have died." The tense denotes, not the act of dying, but the consequences of dying, the state after death. Death itself would not be a gain to Paul, but to be in the presence of his Lord in glory, that would be gain. Translation: *For, so far as I am concerned, to be living, both as to my very existence and my experience, that is Christ, and to have died, is gain.*

### Verse twenty-two

In view of the fact that Paul says that death has no terrors for him, he must assure them that to remain on earth with the encumbrance of sinful flesh, is probably best for them and him. The word "this" refers to the fact of his remaining on earth. It is that in which the fruit of his apostolic ministry is involved and the necessary condition of that fruit being brought forth. Then, if Paul is assured that his continuing to live in the flesh is most fruitful for the Philippian saints, he has nothing to say as to his preference with respect to his living or dying. Translation: *But if for me life in the flesh be my portion, this very thing (namely, life in the flesh) is that in which the fruit of my ministry will be involved, and is the condition of that fruit being brought forth. Then, what I shall prefer for myself, I do not make known.*

### Verses twenty-three and twenty-four

The expression, "I am in a strait betwixt two," could be variously translated. "I am hemmed in on both sides by the two," or "I am held together by the two so that I cannot incline either way." The definite article appears in the Greek text before "two," the word "two" referring back to the life and death previously mentioned. There is an equal pressure being exerted from both sides, from the desire for continued life and from the desire for death. Paul was perplexed, held in, kept back from decision.

There was a strong pressure bearing upon him from both sides, keeping him erect and motionless.

The word "desire" is in the Greek "a passionate desire." "To depart" is from a Greek word used of loosing a ship from its moorings or of striking one's tent. Probably, the latter figure was in the apostle's mind. He was a tent maker by trade, he spoke of the human body as a tent, and he was a prisoner at the barracks of the Praetorian Guard. The phrase "abide in the flesh," has the idea, "to cling to this present life with all its inconveniences and to stand by a mortal body." Translation: *Rather, I am being held motionless by an equal pull from the two (namely, life and death), so that I cannot incline either way, having the passionate desire towards striking my tent and being with Christ, which is by far better, but still to remain with my flesh is more needful for your sake.*

### Verse twenty-five

The word "confidence" in the Greek means "to persuade," and is in the perfect tense. It speaks of a settled conviction which is the result of a past completed process of turning a matter over in one's mind until one is persuaded of it. Paul had turned over in his mind the need which the Philippian saints had of his ministry, and had come to the settled conviction that they needed him more than he needed to go to heaven just then. That was just like Paul. He lived a crucified life, dead to self, ever setting even his legitimate desires aside in order that he might serve others. Having come to this settled conviction, namely, that they needed him more than he needed to go to heaven right then, he tells them that he will remain on earth with them. While Paul had no active choice in the matter, yet he believed that *the servant of the Lord is immortal until his work is done.* Thus, if the Philippians needed his ministry, that fact would indicate that he was not to die at that time by the hand of Rome, but that he would be released and thus be able to minister to the spiritual needs of the saints.

The word "continue" is the translation of a Greek word having a special sense of remaining alive. "Furtherance" is from the same Greek word we studied in verse twelve, referring to the pioneer advance of the gospel there, and here, to the Christian progress which the Philippians would make under the ministry of the apostle, a progress in new paths of Christian conduct and service which would otherwise not be possible. Translation: *And having come to this settled conviction (namely, that to remain in the flesh is more needful for you), I know that I shall remain and continue alive with you all for your progress and joy in your faith.*

### Verse twenty-six

The progress which the saints would make in their trust in the Lord Jesus, which progressive trust would result in growth in their Christian experience and the joy that would be theirs in their enjoyment of this repose of their faith in their Saviour, would in turn result in their more abundant rejoicing in the Lord Jesus. Christ Jesus is the sphere in which these blessings are enjoyed, the sphere in the sense that He made them possible through the blood of His Cross, and in the sense that He is the joy of the believer's life, the One who completely satisfies. Paul is the human instrument through whom God works to bring these joys to the Philippians by means of his personal presence with them again. The word "coming" is from a Greek word which means "to be beside," and thus has come to mean "personal presence." It is the word used of the coming of the Lord Jesus, both with reference to His coming for His Church and with reference to His second Advent. Translation: *In order that your rejoicing may abound in Christ Jesus through me by reason of my personal presence with you again.*

# 4.

## PAUL EXHORTS THE SAINTS TO LIVE IN A MANNER
## WHICH IS WORTHY OF THE GOSPEL (1:27-30)

### Verse twenty-seven

THE word "only" connects Paul's statement that the assurance which he has that he will be given his freedom, comes from the fact that the Philippian saints need his ministry, with his exhortation to them to conduct themselves worthy of the gospel. Since their need of his ministry is the only reason for his wishing to remain on earth, it behooves the Philippian saints to receive that ministry with an open heart, obey his Spirit-given exhortations, and grow in their Christian experience.

The rest of the letter therefore has to do with the spiritual needs of these saints. As we study these exhortations, we discover what things were lacking in their lives and what things needed to be corrected. The basic, all-inclusive exhortation is, "Let your conversation be as it becometh the gospel of Christ."

The word "conversation" deserves special attention. Today the word refers to the interchange of connected discourse between two or more persons. At the time the Authorized Version was translated, it meant "manner of life," "behavior." While the Greek word from which it is translated means that, yet it means more than that. It is the word *politeuo*. From it we get such words as "politic, political." It referred to the public duties devolving upon a man as a member of a body. Paul uses it in Acts 23:1 where he answers the charge of having violated the laws and customs of the Jewish people and so subverting the theocratic constitution. He says, "I have lived in all good conscience before God until this day." The words "have lived" are the translation of this word. Paul said in effect by the use of this word, "I have fulfilled all the duties devolving upon me as a member of the nation Israel in its relation to God." Polycarp, writing to the Philippians, and using this same word says, "If we perform our duties under Him as simple citizens, He will promote us to a share in His sovereignty." The word "conversation" is the translation in the New Testament of another Greek word *anastrepho*, in such places as II Corinthians 1:12 and Ephesians 2:3, and means "manner of life, behavior." This Greek word means literally "to turn hither and thither, to turn one's self about," and thus has come to refer to one's walk, manner of life, or conduct. But Paul uses a specialized word here which is directly connected with the city of Philippi and its citizens. The word *anastrepho* speaks of one's manner of life considered as such, but the word Paul uses in Philippians speaks of one's manner of life seen as a duty to a body or group of which one is a member, and to the head of that group to whom he is responsible. It is a more inclusive word.

The use of this word has to do with the fact that the city of Philippi was a Roman colony. Lightfoot says of its use: "Appreciating its strategical importance of which he had had recent experience, Augustus founded at Philippi a Roman military colony with the high-sounding name 'Colonia Augusta Julia Philippensis.' At the same time he conferred upon it the special privilege of the 'jus Italicum.' A colony is described by an ancient writer as a miniature likeness of the Roman people; and this character is fully borne out by the account of Philippi in the apostolic narrative. The political atmosphere of the place is wholly Roman. The chief magistrates, more strictly designated duumvirs, arrogate to themselves the loftier title of praetors. Their servants, like the attendant officers of the highest function-

aries in Rome, bear the name of lictors. The pride and privilege
of Roman citizenship confront us at every turn. This is the
sentiment which stimulates the blind loyalty of the people:[1]
that is the power which obtains redress for the prisoners and
forces an apology from the unwilling magistrates.[2]  Nor is this
feature entirely lost sight of, when we turn from St. Luke's narrative to St. Paul's epistle. Addressing a Roman colony from
the Roman metropolis, writing as a citizen to citizens, he recurs
to the political franchise as an apt symbol of the higher privileges
of their heavenly calling, to the political life as a suggestive meta-
phor for the duties of their Christian profession." Paul uses the
word in its noun form in 3:20 where he says, "For our conversation is in heaven," or as one could more fully translate, "For the
commonwealth of which we are citizens has its fixed location in
heaven."

The use of this specialized word colors the entire epistle, and
gives to it a heavenly atmosphere. It teaches us that Christians
are citizens of heaven, having a heavenly origin, and a heavenly
destiny, with the responsibility of living a heavenly life on this
earth in the midst of ungodly people and surroundings, telling
sinners of a Saviour in heaven who will save them from their
sins if they but trust Him. The ethics in the letter are invested
with heavenly standards. The saints are reminded that as a colony
of heaven, they are to live heavenly lives on earth, representing
their Sovereign by a life which reflects Him. They are taught that
obedience to the ethics of the Pauline epistles is not merely obedience to ethics as such, but involves a duty which they are responsible to discharge as citizens of a heavenly kingdom, and as subjects of a heavenly King. The earthly counterpart of this was the
institution of emperor worship, in which the subjects of Rome
were not only obligated to obey the laws as a political duty, but

-----

1.  *Acts* 16:21
2.  *Acts* 16:37-39

to obey them as a religious one, since the emperor was worshipped as a god.

Paul says "Let your conversation be as it becometh the gospel of Christ." The expression could be variously translated: "Behave as citizens." "Live as citizens." "Perform your duties as citizens." It is in the middle voice, which voice is defined as follows: When a verb is in the middle voice, the subject acts upon itself. For instance, "the man is prodding his own conscience." Here, the Philippian saints are exhorted to act upon themselves in recognizing their duties with respect to their heavenly citizenship, and holding themselves to them. It is a stronger exhortation than merely that of commanding someone to do something. In the latter kind of exhortation, the person obeys the one who exhorts. But in the form in which Paul gives the exhortation, the person exhorted is to recognize his position as a citizen of a heavenly kingdom, and while obeying the exhortation as a matter of obligation to God, yet at the same time realize his responsibility to obey it because of the privileged position he occupies, and literally exhort or charge himself to do the same. One could translate therefore: "Only see to it that you recognize your responsibility as a citizen and put yourself to the absolute necessity of performing the duties devolving upon you in that position."

The Greek word translated "becometh" is most interesting. When it is used with the genitive case, it means "having the weight of (weighing as much as) another thing." It means, "of like value, worth as much." Other meanings are "befitting, congruous, corresponding." The saints are to see to it that their manner of life weighs as much as the gospel they profess to believe, or their words will not have weight. That which gives weight to a Christian's words, is the fact that his manner of life befits, is congruous to, corresponds with the gospel he preaches.

In the Greek word translated "stand fast," the ideas of firmness or uprightness are prominent. It means "to stand firm and hold one's ground." The implication is clear that when one holds one's ground, he does it in the face of enemy opposition. They are to stand fast in one spirit. The word "spirit" here refers to the unity of spirit in which the members of the church should be fused and blended. The Greek word "spirit" is used at times of the disposition or influence which fills and governs the soul of anyone. It is so used here. This unity of spirit when present among the members of a local church, is produced by the Holy Spirit.

The word "mind" is the translation of the Greek word "soul." The soul is that part of man which on the one hand receives impressions from the human spirit, and on the other hand, from the outer world. It is the sphere of the emotions, the reason, and the will. It is that in and by which the exertion here spoken of would take place. "Striving" is the translation of a Greek word used of an athletic contest. We get our words "athlete" and "athletics" from it. A prefixed preposition implying co-operation, makes the total meaning of the word refer to an athletic contest in which a group of athletes co-operates as a team against another team, working in perfect co-ordination against a common opposition. Paul is exhorting the members of the Philippian church to work together in perfect co-ordination just like a team of Greek athletes. This illustration was not lost upon the Greek readers of Paul's letter. This is the first intimation in the latter that there were some divisions in the church. Paul had somehow gotten out of a possibly reluctant Epaphroditus, that all was not well in the Philippian church. The words, "the faith," are a technical term referring to Christianity. Translation: *Only (since my only reason for remaining on earth is for your progress in the Christian life), see to it that you recognize your responsibility as citizens (of heaven), and put yourselves to the absolute necessity of performing the duties devolving upon you in that position, doing this in a manner which is befitting to the gospel of Christ, in order that whether having come and having seen you, or whether being absent I am hearing the things concerning you, namely, that you are standing firm in one spirit, holding your ground, with one soul contending (as a team of athletes would) in perfect co-operation with one another for the faith of the gospel.*

## Verse twenty-eight

"Terrified" is from a word used of the terror of a startled horse. The Greek word translated "adversaries" gives us a picture of these enemies of the gospel, namely, "those who are entrenched in their opposition against" you. These were the pagan Greeks at Philippi who were idolators and very devout. These would oppose a faith which forbade idolatry. "Which" refers to the fact of the Philippian saints not being terrified. It has in it a qualitative aspect, emphasizing the nature of the act. The words "evident token" are the translation of a Greek law term, denoting proof obtained by an appeal to facts. Thus the failure of the saints to be terrified by the antagonism of their adversaries, was clear evidence of such a nature as to convince these pagans that they were on the road to utter destruction, and clear evidence of the salvation of the Philippian believers.

The word "that" refers back to the words "evident token." This clear evidence was from God, on the one part to the pagans, on the other to the believers. Vincent connects the words "evident token" with the phrase "that of God;" "Lightfoot finds here an allusion, in accord with striving together, to the sign of life or death given by the populace in the amphitheater when a gladiator was vanquished, by turning the thumbs up or down. 'The Christian gladiator does not anxiously await the signal of life or death from a fickle crowd. The great Director of the contest Himself has given him a sure token of deliverance'." Translation: *And not being affrighted in even one thing by those who are entrenched in their opposition against you, which failure on your part to be frightened is an indication of such a nature as to*

*present clear evidence to them of utter destruction, also clear
evidence of your salvation, and this evidence from God.*

### Verse twenty-nine

The words "it is given" are from the word used of God when
He in grace freely and graciously bestows on believing sinners
the gift of salvation. The words "in the behalf of" are the translation of the Greek preposition used of the substitutionary aspect
of our Lord's death on the Cross. It means not only "for the
sake of," but "in the place of." It has been graciously given
the saints to suffer not only for the sake of but in the place of
Christ. It should be clear that we cannot share in His expiatory
sufferings on the Cross, much less endure those in His stead.
The sufferings to which Paul refers here are Christ's sufferings
for righteousness' sake while on earth in His humiliation.  He
says in Colossians 1:24 that he fills "up that which is behind of
the afflictions of Christ" in his flesh "for His body's sake." Our
Lord's sufferings for righteousness' sake which He endured as a
result of human antagonism against Himself, ended with His death
on the Cross.  He has left with the Church the message of salvation, the preaching of which draws the antagonism of the world.
Thus, as the saints suffer for righteousness' sake, they substitute
for their absent Lord not only in the task of preaching the message He has given them but also in suffering for His sake and
in His stead.

The word "for" connects the words "in nothing terrified" with
"to suffer for his sake." The prospect of suffering was apt to
terrify the Philippian saints, but when they viewed suffering in
its true light, they discovered that it was a gift of God's grace
instead of an evil.  But not only is suffering a gift of God's grace,
but the act of placing one's faith in the Lord Jesus is a gift of
that same grace (Eph. 2:8). Translation: *And the reason why
you should not be terrified is because to you that very thing was
graciously given for the sake of Christ and in His behalf, not only*

*to the believing on Him, but also to be suffering for His sake
and in His behalf.*

### Verse thirty

The word "conflict" is the translation of a Greek word used of
an athletic contest. Our word "agony" comes from it. "Life is
in reality an Olympic festival. We are God's athletes to whom
He has given an opportunity of showing what stuff we are made
of." The word was used in later Greek of an inward struggle.
Paul uses it to describe his own life in the midst of his untiring
work for the Lord Jesus. Translation: *Having the same struggle
which ye saw in me and now hear to be in me.*

## 5

## PAUL HOLDS UP TO THE SAINTS THE EXAMPLE OF THE LORD JESUS (2:1-18)

### Verse one

THE exhortation in 1:27, expressed more in the form of a hope that Paul will hear that the Philippians are standing fast in one spirit and with one mind are striving together for the faith of the gospel, is elaborated upon in 2:2 in the words, "Fulfill ye my joy that ye be likeminded, having the same love, being of one accord, of one mind." This exhortation to unity is given in view of four facts which are stated in 2:1, and should be obeyed by the Philippians because of these four facts.

The word "if" is the translation of a conditional particle referring to a fulfilled condition. One could translate "since," or "in view of the fact." The four things mentioned in this verse are not hypothetical in their nature. They are facts.

The first is that there is a certain consolation in Christ, the word "any" being the translation of the indefinite pronoun in Greek which means "a certain thing." The word "consolation" is the translation of a Greek word which has various meanings; "imploration, supplication, entreaty, exhortation, admonition, encouragement, consolation, comfort, solace," the meaning to be used in any particular case being determined by the context in which the word is used. What these Philippians needed right here was not consolation but exhortation, in view of the lack of unity among them. Our translation reads, "In view of the fact that there is a certain exhortation, admonition, encouragement in Christ." That is, Christ's wonderful life should be an admonition and exhortation and encouragement to the Philippians to live in a state of harmony among themselves. Paul uses this as a basis for his exhortation to them. Thus our fuller translation reads, "In view of the fact therefore that there is a certain ground of appeal in Christ which exhorts, . . . be likeminded."

The word "comfort" is the translation of a Greek word which means literally, "a word which comes to the side of one to stimulate or comfort him." It speaks of persuasive address. Lightfoot translates it by the words "incentive, encouragement." It is almost equivalent to the word rendered "consolation," but has an element of tenderness and persuasion involved in its meaning. The word "love" is the Greek word used of God's love. We have here the subjective genitive construction, in which the noun in the genitive case, "love," produces the action in the noun of action, "comfort." That is, the tender persuasion and encouragement which exhorts to unity among the Philippians, comes from God's love for them. Their realization of divine love which reached down and saved them, should urge them to live in a spirit of unity with one another. In addition to that, this divine love produced in the hearts of the Philippian saints by the Holy Spirit, should cause them to so love each other with a love that impels one to sacrifice one's self for the one loved, that their little differences will be ironed out, and they will live in unity with one another. We translate, "since there is a certain tender persuasion that comes from divine love."

Then there is a certain fellowship of the Spirit. The Greek word translated "fellowship,"[1] speaks of a common interest and a mutual and active participation in the things of God in which the believer and the Holy Spirit are joint-participants. This is the result of the Spirit's work of regeneration and His control over

---

1. *Riches*, pp. 96-102

the saint who is definitely subjected to Him. Paul appeals to the Philippians to be likeminded in view of the fact that each of them participates with the Holy Spirit in a common interest and activity, and therefore, if each saint is interested in the things of the Spirit, and thus in the same things, there should naturally follow a unity among the Philippians. The Holy Spirit by thus controlling each saint, produces this unity and accord amongst them.

One might ask here, "If each saint is indwelt by the Spirit, why is there not that unity among the saints, of which Paul speaks?" The answer is, that this joint-participation in an interest and a mutual and active participation in the things of God is produced by the Spirit, not by virtue of His indwelling but by virtue of His control over the believer. The trouble in the Philippian church was that all the saints were not living Spirit-filled lives. If they had been, there would have been unity. Paul's exhortation to unity among the Philippian saints was therefore given upon a reasonable and workable basis. There could be unity if they would all live Spirit-controlled lives. Our fuller translation is: "In view of the fact that there is a certain joint-participation with the Spirit in a common interest and activity, . . . be likeminded."

The fourth reason why the Philippians should live in harmony with one another is that there are certain "bowels and mercies." The word "bowels" we treated in 1:8. It means here "tenderheartednesses." "Mercies" could also be rendered "compassionate yearnings and actions." These graces present in the lives of the Philippian saints would move them to live at peace with one another. Little differences would be patched up. Estrangements would be healed. Bickerings would cease. Translation: *In view of the fact that there is a certain ground of appeal in Christ which exhorts, since there is a certain tender persuasion that comes from divine love, in view of the fact that there is a certain joint-participation with the Spirit in a common interest and activity, since*

*there are certain tenderheartednesses and compassionate yearn-*
*ings and actions.*

### Verse two

"Fulfil" is to be taken in the sense of "complete, fill full." "Be likeminded," literally, "think the same thing," refers to the general concord that should exist among them. This is defined and shown in its three constituent elements, "having the same love," unity of affection, "being of one accord," literally, "soul with soul," unity of sentiment, and "of one mind," literally, "thinking the one thing," the last expression being repetition in stronger terms. Here we have what is called "the tautology of earnestness." These exhortations refer to the same point of view in common interests. Minute distinctions must not be forced. Translation: *Fill full my joy by thinking the same thing, having the same love, being in heart agreement, thinking the one thing.*

### Verse three

"Through" in the Greek indicates the regulative state of mind. It shows the impelling motive. "Strife" has the idea of factiousness. There were factions in the Philippian church, as this exhortation infers. The prohibitions in the Pauline epistles are an indication of what is wrong in the situation which the apostle wishes to correct. "Vain glory" is the translation of a word made up of two words, one word meaning "empty," or "vain," used in the sense of "to no purpose, futile," and the other meaning "opinion." Thus the total meaning is "empty pride." "Lowliness" is the translation of the word translated in other places "humble, humility." Plato defines it as follows: "That state of mind which submits to the divine order of the universe, and does not impiously exalt itself." In pagan writers generally, the word had a bad meaning, "abject, grovelling." But when it comes into the New Testament, its meaning is ennobled. The word is used in a secular document, of the Nile River at its low stage, in the sentence, "It runs low."

"Esteem" is from a word referring to a belief that rests, not on one's inner feelings or sentiment, but on the due consideration of external grounds, on the weighing and comparing of facts. "Better" is the translation of a word which means literally "having above," thus "to excel or surpass." Translation: *Doing nothing impelled by a spirit of factiousness, nothing impelled by empty pride, but in lowliness of mind consider one another as excelling themselves, this estimation resting, not upon feelings or sentiment, but upon a due consideration of facts.*

### Verse four

"Look" is from a Greek word which means "to fix the attention upon with desire for and interest in." Lightfoot renders it, "to consult one's own interest." *Expositor's Greek Testament* translates, "No party having an eye for its own interests alone but also for the rest." Translation: *Not consulting each one his own interests only, but also each one the interests of others.*

### Verse five

After exhorting the Philippian saints in 2:2-4 to think the same thing, to have the same love, to be in heart agreement, and in lowliness of mind to consider one another as excelling themselves, Paul says, "Let this mind be in you which was also in Christ Jesus." *This exhortation reaches back to 2:2-4 for its definition and ahead to 2:6-8 for its illustration.* Paul does not give all that is in the mind of Christ in these verses. He selects those qualities of our Lord which fit the needs of the Philippians at that moment. That which Paul speaks of as being in the mind of Christ and which the Philippians were to include in their own spiritual lives consisted of a spirit of humility and of self-abnegation and an interest in the welfare of others. These graces were illustrated in our Lord's act of becoming incarnate in the human race and becoming the substitutionary atonement for sin. This lack of unity among the Philippian saints became the occasion for perhaps the greatest Christological passage in the New Testament that sounds the depths of the incarnation. Among scholars it is known as the *Kenosis* passage, speaking of the self-emptying of the Son of God as He became incarnate in humanity, the word *kenosis* being the Greek word meaning "to empty."

The Greek word order for the expression just noted is, "This be ye constantly thinking in you which also was in Christ Jesus." The position of the pronoun "this" is emphatic and shows that the exhortation reaches back basically to 2:2-4, while the pronoun "who" in 2:6 connects the exhortation with the illustration in 2:5-8. The words "let mind be" are the translation of one Greek word which means, "to have understanding, to be wise, to direct one's mind to a thing, to seek or strive for." The word seems always to keep in view the direction which thought of a practical kind takes. The expression could be translated in a number of ways, each of which while holding to the main idea, yet brings out a slightly different shade of meaning. For instance: "Be constantly thinking this in yourselves;" "Be having this mind in you;" "Reflect in your own minds, the mind of Christ Jesus" (Lightfoot); "Let the same purpose inspire you as was in Christ Jesus" (Way). The sum total of the thought in the exhortation seems to be that of urging the Philippians to emulate in their own lives, the distinctive virtues of the Lord Jesus spoken of in 2:2-4. It is the habitual direction of our Lord's mind with reference to self that is in the apostle's thinking, an attitude of humility and self-abnegation for the benefit of others, which should be true also of the Philippians. This gives us the key to unlock the rich treasures of the great doctrinal portion of the letter we are now to study. As to the translation of the verse, we might say that the verb of being is not in the Greek text. It is often left out by the writer, and supplied by the reader. In the case of the Authorized Version, we have the word "was." It could just as well be "is," for the Lord Jesus still has that same mind. But the past tense verb "was" suits the context better since the apostle is speaking of the past act of supreme renunciation performed by our Lord in His incarnation and atoning sacrifice. Translation: *This mind be constantly having in you which was also in Christ Jesus.*

### Verse six

The first word which we must carefully study is "form." The Greek word has no reference to the shape of any physical object. It was a Greek philosophical term. Vincent has an excellent note on the word. In discussing it, he has among other things, the following to say: "We must here dismiss from our minds the idea of shape. The word is used in its philosophical sense to denote that expression of being which carries in itself the distinctive nature and character of the being to whom it pertains, and is thus permanently identified with that nature and character . . . As applied to God, the word is intended to describe that mode in which the essential being of God expresses itself. We have no word which can convey this meaning, nor is it possible for us to formulate the reality. *Form* inevitably carries with it to us the idea of *shape*. It is conceivable that the essential personality of God may express itself in a mode apprehensible by the perception of pure spiritual intelligences; but the mode itself is neither apprehensible nor conceivable by human minds.

"This mode of expression, this *setting* of the divine essence, is not *identical* with the essence itself, but is *identified with it* as its natural and appropriate expression, answering to it in every particular. It is the perfect expression of a perfect essence. It is not something imposed from without, but something which proceeds from the very depth of the perfect being, and into which that being unfolds, as light from fire."

Thus the Greek word for "form" refers to that outward expression which a person gives of his inmost nature. This expression is not assumed from the outside, but proceeds directly from within. To illustrate: "I went to a tennis match yesterday. The winning player's form was excellent." We mean by that, that the outward expression he gave of his inward ability to play tennis, was excellent. The expression in this case took the form of the rhythmic, graceful, swift, and coordinated movements of his body and its members.

Our Lord was in the form of God. The word "God" is without the definite article in the Greek text, and therefore refers to the divine essence. Thus, our Lord's outward expression of His inmost being was as to its nature the expression of the divine essence of Deity. Since that outward expression which this word "form" speaks of, comes from and is truly representative of the inward being, it follows that our Lord as to His nature is the possessor of the divine essence of Deity, and being that, it also necessarily follows that He is absolute Deity Himself, a co-participant with God the Father and God the Holy Spirit in that divine essence which constitutes God, God.

The time at which the apostle says our Lord gave expression to His essential nature, that of Deity, was previous to His coming to earth to become incarnate as the Man Christ Jesus. But Paul, by the use of the Greek word translated "being," informs his Greek readers that our Lord's possession of the divine essence did not cease to be a fact when He came to earth to assume human form. The Greek word is not the simple verb of being, but a word that speaks of an antecedent condition protracted into the present. That is, our Lord gave expression to the essence of Deity which He possesses, not only before He became Man, but also after becoming Man, for He was doing so at the time this Philippian epistle was being written. To give expression to the essence of Deity implies the possession of Deity, for this expression, according to the definition of our word "form," comes from one's inmost nature. *This word alone is enough to refute the claim of Modernism that our Lord emptied Himself of His Deity when He became Man.*

This expression of the essence of His Deity which our Lord gave in His pre-incarnate state, was given through a spiritual medium to spiritual intelligences, the angels. Human beings in their present state of being cannot receive such impressions, since they are not equipped with the spiritual sense of perception which the angels have. What Peter, James, and John saw on the Mount of Transfiguration was an outward expression of the essence of Deity, but given through a medium by which the physical senses of the disciples could receive the expression given. But when believers receive their bodies of glory, they will be equipped to receive the expression of Deity which the angels received, and through a like spiritual medium.

Now, at this time, in the eternity before the universe was created, Paul says that our Lord "thought it not robbery to be equal with God." The word translated "thought" refers to a judgment based upon facts. The word "God" is used again without the article. Had the article preceded it, the meaning would be "equal with God the Father." The word "God" here refers to Deity, not seen in the three Persons of the Godhead, but to Deity seen in its essence. Equality with God does not refer here to the equality of the Lord Jesus with the other Persons of the Trinity. Nor does it refer to His equality with them in the *possession* of the divine essence. Possession of the divine essence is not spoken of here, but the *expression* of the divine essence is referred to, although *possession* is implied by the *expression*. Equality with God here refers to our Lord's co-participation with the other members of the Trinity in the expression of the divine essence. This is a very important point, for when we come to consider the fact that our Lord laid aside something, we will see that it was not the *possession* but the *expression* of the divine essence.

We must now consider carefully the word "robbery." The Greek word has two distinct meanings, "a thing unlawfully seized," and "a treasure to be clutched and retained at all hazards." When a Greek word has more than one meaning, the rule of interpretation is to take the one which agrees with the context in which it is found. The passage which we are studying is the illustration of the virtues mentioned in 2:2-4, namely, humility, and self-abnegation for the benefit of others. If our Lord did not consider it a thing to be unlawfully seized to be equal with God in the expression of the divine essence, then He would be asserting His rights to that expression. He would be declaring His rightful ownership of that prerogative. But to assert one's right to a thing does not partake of an attitude of humility and self-abnegation. Therefore, this meaning of the word will not do here. If our Lord did not consider the expression of His divine essence such a treasure that it should be retained at all hazards, that would mean that He was willing to waive His rights to that expression if the necessity arose. This is the essence of humility and of self-abnegation. Thus, our second meaning is the one to be used here. Translation. *Who has always been and at present continues to subsist in that mode of being in which He gives outward expression of His essential nature, that of Deity, and who did not after weighing the facts, consider it a treasure to be clutched and retained at all hazards, to be equal with Deity (in the expression of the divine essence);*

### Verse seven

We now consider the words, "made himself of no reputation." Instead of asserting His rights to the expression of the essence of Deity, our Lord waived His rights to that expression, being willing to relinquish them if necessary. He did not consider the exercise of that expression such a treasure that it would keep Him from setting that expression aside, and making Himself of no reputation. The words "made himself of no reputation" are the translation of two Greek words which literally translated mean, "emptied Himself." Before we discuss the question as to what our Lord emptied Himself of, we must examine the words, "and took upon him the form of a servant."

The word "form" is from the same Greek word that we studied in verse six. The word "servant" is the translation of the Greek word which Paul used in 1:1 to describe himself, a bondslave. The word "and" is not in the Greek text, but was supplied by the translators. The word "took" is an aorist participle. A rule of Greek grammar says that the action of an aorist participle precedes the action of the leading verb. The leading verb here is "emptied." That means that the act of taking preceded the act of emptying. That in turn means that the act of taking upon Himself the form of a servant preceded and was the cause of the emptying. The translation so far could read, "emptied Himself, having taken the form of a bondslave."

What do the words mean, "having taken the form of a bondslave?" The word "form," you remember, referred to the outward expression one gives of his inward being. The words "form of a bondslave" therefore mean that our Lord gave outward expression to His inmost nature, the outward expression being that of a bondslave. The words "having taken" tell us that that expression was not true of Him before, although the desire to serve others was part of His nature as Deity. When expressing Himself as a bondslave come to serve, He necessarily exchanged one form of expression for another. In verse six He was in His pre-incarnate state expressing Himself as Deity. In verse seven He expresses Himself in incarnation as a bondslave. This is the direct opposite of what took place at the Transfiguration. There we have the same word "form" used, but with a prefixed preposition signifying a change. We could translate "And the mode of His outward expression was changed before them, and His face did shine as the sun, and His raiment was white as the light" (Matt. 17:2). Our Lord's usual mode of expression while on earth previous to His resurrection was that of a servant. He said, "The son of man came not to be ministered unto, but to minister, and to give his life a ransom for many" (Matt. 20:28). But now, His outward expression as a servant ceased, and He gave outward expression of the glory of His deity. In our Philippian passage, the change of expression is reversed. Instead of giving outward expression of His deity to the angels in His pre-incarnate glory, He gives outward expression of His humility in becoming the servant of mankind. The one expression was set aside so that the other could become a fact. Vincent says in this connection: "This *form*, not being *identical* with the divine essence, but dependent upon it, and necessarily implying it, can be parted with or laid aside. Since Christ is one with God, and therefore pure being, absolute existence, He can exist without the form. This form of God, Christ laid aside in His incarnation." Both expressions came from our Lord's nature, His act of glorifying Himself and His act of humbling Himself. Both are constituent elements of the essence possessed by the Triune God.

But in exchanging one form of expression for the other, He emptied Himself. The question arises, "Of what did He empty Himself?" He did not empty Himself of His deity, since Paul says that the expression of His deity was a fact after His incarnation, that expression implying the possession of the essence of Deity. He set aside the *outward expression* of His deity when expressing Himself as a bondslave. It was the outward expression of the essence of His deity which our Lord emptied Himself of during the time when He was giving outward expression of Himself as a bondslave. But the emptying Himself of the expression of Deity is more implied by the context than stated specifically by the verb "emptied." When our Lord set aside the expression of Deity in order that He might express Himself as a bondslave, He was setting aside His legitimate and natural desires and prerogatives as Deity. The basic, natural desire and prerogative of Deity is that of being glorified. But when Deity sets these aside, it sets its desires aside, and setting its desires aside, it sets Self aside. The pronoun "Himself" is in the accusative case. The action of the verb terminates in the thing expressed by that case. The act of emptying terminated in the self life of the Son of God. Our Lord emptied Himself of self. This agrees perfectly with the context which is an example of humility and self-abnegation for the benefit of others. This setting aside of self by the Son of God was the example that Paul held before the saints at Philippi. If each one would set self aside, then unity would prevail.

An illustration of this self-emptying of the Son of God is found in John 13:1-17. Our Lord seated at the table, the Master and Lord of the disciples, is illustrative of Him in His preincarnate glory, giving outward expression of the glory of His deity to the angels. Our Lord, girded with a towel, and washing the feet of the disciples, is illustrative of His taking the outward expression of a servant in His incarnation. His outer garments laid aside for the time being, point to His setting aside the outward expression of His pre-incarnate glory while He expressed Himself as a bond-slave. The fact that He was still their Master and Lord while kneeling on the floor doing the work of an oriental slave, speaks of the fact that our Lord's assumption of humanity did not mean that He relinquished His deity. He was just as much God while on earth in His humiliation, as He was before He came and as He is now. His act of taking His outer garments again, tells of the resumption of the expression of His glory after the resurrection.

The words "took upon him the form of a servant," do not refer to His assumption of human nature without its sin, but to His expression of Himself as a bondslave. His humanity was only the necessary medium through which He would express Himself as a servant of mankind. The fact of His becoming man is expressed in the words, "and was made in the likeness of men." The words "was made" are the translation of a word meaning "to become." The tense of this verb is ingressive aorist, which signifies entrance into a new state. Our Lord entered into a new state of being when He became Man. But His becoming Man did not exclude His possession of Deity. He was and is today a Person with two natures, that of absolute Deity and that of humanity. The text says, "He became in the likeness of men." The word "likeness" in the Greek text refers to "that which is made like something else." Our Lord's humanity was a real likeness, not a phantom, nor an incomplete copy of humanity. But this likeness did not express the whole of Christ's being. His mode of manifestation resembled what men are. But His humanity was not all that there was of Him. He was also Deity. He was not a man, but the Son of God manifest in the flesh and nature of man. Translation: *But emptied Himself, having taken the outward expression of a bondslave, which expression came from and was truly representative of His nature, entering into a new state of existence, that of mankind.*

### Verse eight

The word "fashion" is the translation of a Greek word that refers to an outward expression that is assumed from the outside and does not come from within. Our Greek word for "form" we found to refer to an outward expression that came from one's inner nature. Our Lord's expression of His Deity was not assumed from the outside, but came from His inmost nature. Likewise, His outward expression as a bondslave came from His inmost nature. But His expression of His humanity came, not from His inmost nature as God, but was assumed in the incarnation. The contrast here is between what He was in Himself, God, and what he appeared in the eyes of men. The word "fashion" therefore referred to that which is purely outward, and appeals to the senses. Our Lord's humanity was real. He was really a Man, but He was not a real man in the sense that He was like others of the human race, only a man. He was always in His incarnation, more than man. There was always that single personality with a dual nature. His deity did not make Him more nor less than a Man, and His humanity did not make Him less than absolute Deity. He became in the likeness of man, and He was found in fashion as a man. "Likeness" states the fact of His real resemblance to men in mode of existence, and "fashion" defines the outward mode and form as it appeared in the eyes of men. But He was not found in fashion as *a* man. The indefinite article should not be in the translation. He was found in outward guise as man, not *a* man. He was not a man but God, although He had assumed human nature yet without its sin.

The word "humbled" means "to make or bring low." The word was used in a secular document when describing the Nile River at its low stage, in the sentence "It (the Nile) runs low." What a description of the Son of God. But this self-humbling does not refer to the self-emptying of verse seven. That was a self-humbling in His character as God the Son. Here the self-humbling is the act of our Lord as the Son of Man. It was the humiliation of the death of a cross. If it was humiliating to our Lord in His humanity, how much more was it so in His deity.

He became obedient unto death. But this does not mean that He became obedient to death. He was always the Master of death. He died as no other individual ever died or ever will die. He died of His own volition. He dismissed His human spirit. The word "unto" is the translation of a Greek word which means "up to the point of." Our Lord was obedient to the Father up to the point of dying. He said, "Lo, I come to do thy will, O God" (Heb. 10:9). There is no definite article before the word "cross" in the Greek text. There should be none in the translation. That which the apostle wishes to bring out by the absence of the article is the character of His death. It was the death of a cross, its nature, one of ignominy and degradation. It was the kind of death meted out to criminals, and only to those who were not citizens of the Roman Empire. Translation: *And being found to be in outward guise as man, He stooped very low, having become obedient to the extent of death, even such a death as that upon a cross.*

### Verses nine to eleven

"Wherefore," that is, because of this voluntary act of humility, God also highly exalted Him. "Also" marks the correspondence between His self-renunciation and His consequent exaltation by God the Father. The words "highly exalted" are the translation of a Greek word which means "to exalt to the highest rank and power, to raise to supreme majesty." It refers to a super-eminent exaltation.

The word "given" is the translation of the Greek word used when God in grace freely gives salvation to the believing sinner. It is so used in Romans 8:32. It was an act of grace on the part of God the Father toward the incarnate Son who had voluntarily assumed a subordinate position so as to function as the Sin-bearer on the Cross. Vincent translates it, "freely bestowed;" Lightfoot, "gave;" and Thayer, "graciously given."

That which was graciously bestowed was not "a name," but "the Name." The definite article appears in the Greek text and refers to a particular name. The title, THE NAME, is a very common Hebrew title, denoting office, rank, dignity. The expression, "The Name of God" in the Old Testament, denotes the divine Presence, the divine Majesty, especially as the object of adoration and praise. The context here dwells upon the honor and worship bestowed on Him upon whom this name was conferred. The conferring of this title "The Name," was upon the Lord Jesus as the Son of Man. A Man, the Man Christ Jesus, who as Very God had voluntarily laid aside His expression of the glory of Deity during His incarnation, now has placed upon His shoulders all the majesty, dignity, and glory of Deity itself. It is the God-Man who stooped to the depths of humiliation, who is raised, not as God now, although He was all that, but as Man, to the infinite height of exaltation possessed only by Deity. It is the answer of our Lord's prayer "And now, O Father, glorify thou me with thine own self with the glory which I had with thee before the world was" (John 17:5). It is the glory of Deity, not now seen shining in infinite splendor as in His pre-incarnate state, but that glory shining in perfect contrast to and with His glorified humanity raised now to a place of equal dignity with Deity. It is the ideal and beautiful combination of the exaltation of Deity and the humility of Deity seen in incarnate Deity.

We come now to the expression, "that at the name of Jesus every knee should bow." But it is not at the name "Jesus" that every knee will bow. "Jesus" was the name given our Lord at His humiliation. It is at THE NAME that belongs to Jesus that every knee will bow. Every knee will bow in recognition of all that Jesus is in His exaltation. The word "that" is in the Greek literally "in." It is *in* The Name that every knee will bow. The Name is the spiritual sphere, the holy element as it were, in which every prayer will be offered and every knee will bow.

All creation will render such homage, whether animate or inanimate, whether in heaven, on earth, or under the earth. "Confess" is from a Greek word which means "to openly or plainly confess." The word means "to confess" in the sense of "to agree with someone." Some day, the entire universe will agree with God the Father on the testimony which He has given of His Son. The word means also, "to publicly declare." It is used frequently in the Septuagint, and has the ideas of praise or thanksgiving associated with it. The word "Lord" is the translation of a word found in the Greek translation of the Old Testament, where it is used to translate the august title of God, Jehovah. Translation: *Because of which voluntary act of supreme self-renunciation, God also super-eminently exalted Him to the highest rank and power, and graciously bestowed upon Him* THE NAME, *the one which is above every name, in order that in recognition of* THE NAME *belonging to Jesus, every knee should bow, of things in heaven, of things on earth, and of things under the earth, and in order that every tongue should plainly and openly declare that Jesus Christ is* LORD, *resulting in the glory of God the Father.*

### Verses twelve and thirteen

"Wherefore," goes back to 1:27 where Paul's presence and absence are referred to as in this verse. In 1:27 we have Paul's exhortation to the Philippian saints to conduct themselves as citizens of heaven should. Then the apostle singles out one of the obligations of a citizen of heaven, that of living in harmony and unity with his fellow-saints. In 2:1-4, he gives four reasons which in themselves are enablements, why they should live in unity together, and further develops the theme of Christian unity. In 2:5, he tells them that such unity is one of the constituent elements in the mind of Christ, and in 2:6-8, he shows how Christ Jesus exhibited the basic quality of unity, namely, humility and self-abnegation in His incarnation and vicarious death on the Cross, which act on His part was recognized by God the Father in that He exalted His Son as the Man Christ Jesus, placing Him in the place of highest honor in the universe.

Now, in 2:12, 13, the apostle exhorts these saints to make the humility and self-abnegation exhibited by the Lord Jesus, a fact in their own lives. He calls them, "my beloved ones," the word being plural in the Greek. The distinctive word here for "love" refers to the love that God is, to the love produced in the heart by the Holy Spirit, a love that impels one to sacrifice one's self for the benefit of others. This is the heavenly love with which the great apostle loved the Philippians. He commends them for their constant obedience. Then he exhorts them to work out their own salvation. Let us be clear first of all as to what this exhortation does not mean. It does not mean to work *for* one's salvation, and for two reasons; first, Paul was writing to those who were already saved, and second, salvation is not a work of man for God, but a work of God for man, a work that was accomplished at the Cross. Neither does it mean to work out an inworked salvation. The idea of working out an inworked salvation is merely a play upon the English words "work out," and has no support from the Greek.

The words "work out" are the translation of a Greek word which means "to carry out to the goal, to carry to its ultimate conclusion." We say, "The student worked out a problem in arithmetic." That is, he carried the problem to its ultimate conclusion. This is the way it is used here. The Philippians are exhorted to carry their salvation to its ultimate conclusion, namely,

Christlikeness. The salvation spoken of here is not justification, but sanctification, victory over sin and the living of a life pleasing to the Lord Jesus. They are to see to it that they make progress in their Christian lives. They are to do this with fear and trembling. This is not a slavish terror, but a wholesome caution. "This fear is self-distrust; it is tenderness of conscience; it is vigilance against temptation; it is the fear which inspiration opposes to high-mindedness in the admonition, 'be not high-minded but fear.' It is taking heed lest we fall; it is a constant apprehension of the deceitfulness of the heart, and of the insidiousness and power of inward corruption. It is the caution and circumspection which timidly shrinks from whatever would offend and dishonor God and the Saviour" (Vincent, quoting Wardlaw *On Proverbs*). This is human responsibility.

In verse thirteen we have divine enablement. The saints are to carry their salvation which God has given them and which thus belongs to them, to its ultimate goal, always remembering and depending upon the fact that it is God who is working in them both to will and to do of His good pleasure. The word "worketh" in the Greek means "to energize, to work effectively." Our words "energy" and "energize" come from it. The words "to will" are the translation of a Greek word meaning "to desire," and refer to a desire that comes from one's emotions rather than from one's reason. It is this desire to do the good pleasure of God that is produced by divine energy in the heart of the saint as he definitely subjects himself to the Holy Spirit's ministry. It is God the Holy Spirit who energizes the saint, making him not only willing, but actively desirous of doing God's sweet will. But He does not merely leave the saint with the desire to do His will. He provides the necessary power to do it. This we have in the words "to do." The Greek construction implies habit, the habitual doing of God's will.

In verse twelve, we have human responsibility, in verse thirteen, divine enablement, a perfect balance which must be kept if the Christian life is to be lived at its best. It is not a *"let go and let God"* affair. It is a *"take hold with God"* business. It is a mutual co-operation with the Holy Spirit in an interest and an activity in the things of God. The saint must not merely rest in the Holy Spirit for victory over sin and the production of a holy life. He must in addition to this dependence upon the Spirit, say a positive NO to sin and exert himself to the doing of the right. Here we have that incomprehensible and mysterious interaction between the free will of man and the sovereign grace of God. Translation: *Wherefore, my beloved ones, as ye have always obeyed, not as in my presence only, but now much more in my absence, carry to its ultimate conclusion your own salvation with fear and trembling, for God is the One who is constantly putting forth His power in you, both in the form of the constant activity of (your) being desirous of and the constant activity of (your) putting into operation His good pleasure.*

## Verses fourteen and fifteen

One of the ways in which this lack of harmony among the Philippian saints was manifesting itself, was in murmurings and disputings. Paul had somehow gotten that fact out of an Epaphroditus whose love for his brethren back home had led him to cover up their sins. Paul exhorts them to be done with these. The word "murmurings" is the translation of a Greek word which means, "to mutter, to murmur." It was used of the cooing of doves. It is an onomatopoetic word, that is, a word whose sound resembles its meaning. It is spelled, *gongusmon*. It refers, not to a loud outspoken dissatisfaction, but to that undertone murmuring which one sometimes hears in the lobbies of our present day churches where certain cliques are "having it out," so to speak, among themselves. The word refers to the act of murmuring against men, not God. The use of this word shows that the divisions among the Philippians had not yet risen to the point of loud dissension. The word was used of those who confer secretly, of those who discontentedly complain. The word is found in a secular document reporting an interview between Marcus Aurelius and a rebel. A veteran present interposes with the remark, "Lord, while you are sitting in judgment, the Romans are murmuring."

The word "disputings" is the translation of a Greek word that carries the ideas of discussion or debate, with the underthought of suspicion or doubt. The murmurings led to disputes.

The words "may be" are more properly, "may become," implying that they were not blameless at that time. They were not harmless when there were such divisions among them. The Greek word "blameless," has the idea of "blameless, deserving no censure, free from fault or defect." "Harmless" in the Greek text has the idea of "unmixed, unadulterated." It was used of wine without water, and metal without alloy. It means "guileless." "Sons" is more properly "children" or "born ones." "Without rebuke" has the idea of "without blemish, faultless, unblamable."

"Crooked" in the Greek has the idea of "crooked, perverse, wicked," in the sense of turning away from the truth. "Perverse" has the idea of "distorted, having a twist." It is a stronger word than "crooked." "Shine" refers to the fact of appearing, not the act of shining. The word for "lights" is the translation of the Greek word used of the heavenly bodies such as the stars. How appropriate to speak of the saints as luminaries, since they are heavenly people. Translation: *All things be constantly doing without discontented and secret mutterings and grumblings, and without discussions which carry an undertone of suspicion or doubt, to the end that ye may become those who are deserving of no censure, free from fault or defect, and guileless in their simplicity, children of God without blemish, in the midst of a perverse and distorted generation, among whom ye appear as luminaries in the world.*

## Verse sixteen

The words "holding forth" are the translation of a Greek word used in secular documents of offering wine to a guest. It means "to hold forth so as to offer." This should ever be the attitude of the saint, offering salvation to a lost and a dying world. The word "rejoice" is not from the usual Greek word translated "rejoice," but from a word which means "to boast," or "to glory." The word "that," has the idea of "because." The day of Christ refers to the Rapture of the Church. The word "labored" means "to labor to the point of exhaustion." If the Philippians would continue to hold forth the Word, Paul would have ground for glorying when the Lord Jesus comes for His saints, for he would not have run his Christian race in vain nor would he have bestowed exhausting labor on the Philippians in vain, for the results of his efforts in Philippi would be apparent in the soul-winning activities of the saints there. Translation: *Holding forth the Word of life, to the end that I may have a ground for glorying reserved for the day of Christ, this glorying being because of the fact that I have not run in vain nor have I labored to the point of exhaustion in vain.*

## Verses seventeen and eighteen

The words "offered up" are the translation of a Greek word used in the pagan Greek religions, of the drink-offering poured out upon the sacrifice itself, the latter being the major part of the offering to the gods, and the former, the minor part. Paul uses this drink-offering or libation to speak of the violent death he will some day die as a martyr. It will be his blood poured out. Indeed, during his second Roman imprisonment, knowing that he would shortly be sent to the executioner's block for decapitation, he writes to Timothy, using the same word, "For I am now ready to be offered," or as one could translate, "For my life's blood is already being poured out" (II Tim. 4:6).

He uses the main sacrifice as an illustration of the Philippian saint's Christian life and service. The Greek word for "sacrifice" used here was used for both pagan animal sacrifices, and in the Septuagint, for the Old Testament sacrifices. What humility for the great apostle to rejoice at the fact that some day he would be the lesser part of the sacrifice poured out upon the major part, the Philippian's Christian testimony and service to God. The word "service" is from a Greek word used of the religious service of the Old Testament priests. Translation: *In fact, if also I am being poured out as a libation upon the sacrifice and priestly service of your faith, I rejoice and continue to rejoice with you all. But as for you, you even be rejoicing in the same thing and continue to rejoice with me.*

# 6.

## PAUL BRINGS BEFORE THEM THE EXAMPLE OF TIMOTHY (2:19-24)

### Verses nineteen to twenty-four

AFTER presenting the example of our Lord, Paul brings Timothy to the attention of the Philippians. He says, "I trust in the Lord to send Timothy." The phrase "in the Lord" tells us that Paul's every thought, word, and deed proceeded from the Lord as the center of his volition. Pauls says in effect, "My hope is not an idle one, but one that is founded on faith in the Lord." "Timotheus" is the English letter equivalents of the Greek name, and so appears in the Authorized Version. The Anglicized form is of course "Timothy." The words "good comfort" are the translation of a Greek word which means literally "well-souled." It speaks of the well-being of one's soul. The phrase could be translated, "that I also may take courage and be of good cheer." The words "no man" are literally, "not even one." Paul speaks with severity of a disposition so opposed to his own or to that of Timothy. The word "likeminded" is the translation of a Greek word made up of the words "equal" and "soul." The Greek word for "mind" is not used here. Paul says that he does not have a person in Rome with a soul equal to Timothy's. "Like-souled" would be the translation. "Who" has a qualitative aspect in the Greek, namely, "who is of a character such that." "Naturally" in the Greek text has the ideas of "genuinely, faithfully, sincerely," as opposed to "spurious." That is, Timothy was "all wool and a yard wide." He was the genuine article. He could be depended upon. "Care for" is from a word which has the following ideas, "give one's thought to a matter, seek to promote one's interests." Thus Timothy could be depended upon to have a real concern about the welfare of the Philippians.

The words "All seek their own, not the things of Jesus Christ's," do not mean that Paul had no genuine Christian friends in Rome, but that all shrank from visiting far distant Philippi. The word "all" is strong. It means "the whole of them, one and all, all without exception."

The word "proof" refers to that which has met the test and has been approved. Thus, Timothy's approved character is what the word "proof of him" has reference to. "Ye know" is from the Greek word speaking of knowledge gained by experience. The Philippian saints knew Timothy personally. Paul's use of the preposition "with," shows his humility. Timothy was Paul's assistant. He was also Paul's spiritual child. He could have said, "as a son to a father, he hath served me in the gospel." The Greek makes it plain that Paul said "as a son to a father," not "as a son with a father." But instead, in lowliness of mind, he mentions him as a fellow-servant in the Lord. The word "in" is in the Greek text a preposition of motion. It was in the progress of the gospel that Timothy served with Paul.

The word "see" gives us another glimpse into the character of the great apostle. The Greek word speaks here of the act of turning one's attention from other things and concentrating them upon one's own situation. Paul was so forgetful of self, yes, so dead to self, so engrossed in the welfare of others, that, even though he was a prisoner, and was facing martyrdom, yet he had not taken thought of his own welfare. He voices the hope that he will be able to send Timothy soon. But his sending Timothy is dependent upon his own circumstances which may or may not hinder. The word "trust" in the Greek text is not the usual word for "trust," but one that means "to persuade."

It is in the perfect tense. Thus, Paul had come to a settled persuasion. This settled persuasion was in the sphere of the Lord, that is, Paul's convictions in the matter were based on the Lord's faithfulness to him. Translation: *But I am hoping in the Lord quickly to send Timothy to you, in order that I also may be of good cheer, having come to know of your circumstances. For not even one do I have who is like-souled, one of such a character who would genuinely and with no secondary regard for himself be concerned about the welfare of your circumstances. For one and all without exception are constantly seeking their own things, not the things of Jesus Christ. But you know by experience his character which has been approved after having been tested, that as a child to a father, with me he has served in the furtherance of the gospel. Him therefore I am hoping to send as soon as, having turned my attention from other things and having concentrated it upon my own situation, I shall have ascertained my position. But I have come to a settled conviction, which conviction is in the Lord, that I also myself shall come shortly.*

Thus Paul paints for the Philippians the portrait of Timothy, dependable, self-forgetful, genuine in character, "all wool and a yard wide," and unconsciously exhibits some of his own fine qualities also.

**7.**

## PAUL SPEAKS OF THE CHARMING TESTIMONY OF
## EPAPHRODITUS (2:25-30)

*Verse twenty-five*

EPAPHRODITUS is the next example which Paul brings forward who also illustrates in his life the exhortations of 2:1-4. His name means "charming." And what a charming winsome person he was. Paul uses four words to describe him, "brother, companion, fellow-soldier, and messenger." The Greek word "brother," means literally, "from the same womb." It speaks of a common origin. A common origin speaks of a common level. The great apostle puts himself on a common level with this humble brother in Christ who was the Philippians' messenger to Paul. Thus it is that Christianity levels off artificial earthly distinctions and places all, rich and poor, nobility and peasantry, wise and unlearned, on the same level, yes, but on what level? It places all believers on the highest plane, namely, in heavenly places in Christ Jesus. It levels off the distinction between nobility and peasantry, abolishing both so far as our heavenly citizenship is concerned, and creates an aristocracy of which all are members, the aristocracy of heaven.

Then he calls him his fellow-worker. Next he refers to him as his fellow-soldier in the Christian conflict against the powers of darkness. Finally, Paul calls him the messenger of the Philippians. The word "messenger" is the translation of a Greek word that is usually translated "apostle," as in Galatians 1:1. It was used of an ambassador sent on a commission. In using this word, the apostle clothes the messenger service of Epaphroditus with the dignity of an ambassador. But that is not all. The word "ministered" is the translation of a Greek word used of the ritualistic service of the Levitical priests. The service of Epaphroditus in minstering to the needs of Paul while the former was in Rome, was looked upon by the apostle as a ministry having as much sacredness about it as one would meet with in the ministry of the priests in the Jewish temple services.

Paul supposed it necessary to send Epaphroditus back to the Philippians. The word "necessary" in the Greek text is a very strong word. It means "indispensable, what one cannot do without." "Supposed" is the translation of a word that does not contain a doubt, but refers to a decision arrived at after weighing the facts in the case. Translation: *But after weighing the facts, I considered it indispensable to send to you Epaphroditus, my brother and fellow-worker and fellow-soldier, but your ambassador to whom you entrusted a mission, and he who in a sacred way ministered to my needs.*

### Verse twenty-six

The reason why Paul deemed it an absolute necessity to send Epaphroditus back to the Philippians, was because the latter was homesick. Paul says, "He longed after you all." The Greek construction shows that this was not a spasmodic yearning but a continuous one. The words "full of heaviness" are from a Greek word used only two other times in the New Testament (Matt. 26:37 and Mk. 14:33), both of which refer to our Lord's heaviness of soul in Gethsemane. The Greek word finds its origin in a word that has the idea of "not at home," thus, "uncomfortable, troubled, distressed." The word does not refer to homesickness, but to the discomfort of not being at home. Thus the heart of Epaphroditus was not at rest. The reason for this restlessness was that he was concerned that the Philippians had heard of his illness and were themselves concerned over their messenger for whom they in a measure held themselves responsible.  What a miracle divine grace had wrought in the hearts of these Greeks who had recently come up out of rank paganism!  Translation: *For he was constantly yearning after you, and was in sore anguish because you heard that he was sick.*

## Verses twenty-seven to thirty

The words "nigh unto," in the Greek tell us how near Epaphroditus was to death, just next door.  He and death were next door neighbors.  The word means literally, "alongside of a neighbor."  The words "the more carefully" in the Greek have the ideas of "haste," and "diligence."  "Receive" is the translation of a verb which means "to receive to one's self, to give access to one's self."  The prefixed preposition in its root meaning signifies "facing," and this implies fellowship.  The exhortation indicates that there had been some alienation between Epaphroditus and the Philippians.  The word "reputation" is the translation of a Greek word which means "to hold one dear or in honor, to value highly, to prize, to deem precious."  "Not regarding" in the Greek text is a term used in gambling circles.  It means, "to throw down a stake, to venture."  Its adjective means "rash, reckless."  The word was used of brotherhoods who at the risk of their lives nursed the sick and buried the dead.  Epaphroditus had recklessly exposed his life.

That which had brought this servant of the Lord to the door of death was his work of ministering to the apostle.  He supplied the Philippians' lack of service toward Paul in that the former were separated by many miles from their beloved spiritual father and thus could not minister personally to his needs.  But the comforts of his own hired house near the barracks of the Praetorian Guard would not have made necessary such over-exertion on the part of Epaphroditus.  The probability is that Paul was now confined to a prison, the discomforts of which were somewhat relieved by the strenuous labors of Epaphroditus. Translation: *For truly he was ill, next door to death. But God had mercy upon him, and not upon him alone, but also on me, in order that I might not have sorrow upon sorrow. With increased haste and diligence therefore I sent him, in order that having seen him again, you may recover your cheerfulness, and my sorrow may be lessened. Receive him to yourselves therefore with all joy, and hold such ones in honor, value them highly, and deem them precious, because on account of the work of Christ he drew near to death, having recklessly exposed his life in order that he might supply that which was lacking in your service to me.*

## 8

## PAUL, USING HIMSELF AS AN EXAMPLE, WARNS THE
## SAINTS AGAINST THE JUDAIZERS (3:1-14)

### Verse one

PAUL'S "finally" here is not the "finally" of the present day preacher. He has another "finally" in 4:8. He does not mean by this that he is about to close his letter. The words translated by the word "finally" are literally "as for the rest." In every case, the use of this Greek expression has the idea of something left over. Paul has been concerned so far in the letter with the internal dissensions, mild though they were, that endangered the well-being of the Philippian church. Now he turns his attention to a danger that would assail it from without, namely, the Judaizers. These were Jews who were nominal Christians, who accepted the Lord Jesus as the Saviour of Israel only, and who taught that a Gentile had to come through the gate of Judaism in order to be saved. They thus refused to accept the fact of the setting aside of Israel at the Cross, and the bringing in of the Church at Pentecost. They wished to continue under the Mosaic law. What happened in the Galatian churches, Paul was trying to forestall in the church at Philippi.

His first exhortation was designed as a positive preventive of becoming entangled in this false teaching. "Go on constantly rejoicing in the Lord." The Judaizers were rejoicing and boasting in man and his attainments (Gal. 6:12), but Paul said that he would glory only in the Lord Jesus (Gal. 6:14). The words "the same things" refer to former warnings addressed to the Philippian saints against these dangerous teachers who would lead them astray. Translation: *As for the rest (of which I wish to say to you), go on constantly rejoicing in the Lord. To go on writing the same things to you is not to me irksome or tedious, while for you it is safe.*

## Verses two and three

The Greek word translated "beware" has the idea of "constantly observing with a view to avoiding, constantly be looking at in the sense of bewaring." The word "dogs" was a term of reproach among both Greeks and Jews. The poet Homer uses it of men and women, implying recklessness in the former, and shamelessness in the latter. Gentiles of the Christian era were called dogs by the Jews. Our Lord in Matthew 15:26 does not use the word which Paul uses, but instead, a diminutive form of the word. The dogs here were the mangy, flea-bitten, vicious, starved scavengers of the oriental streets, while the dogs our Lord referred to were the well-cared for little house pets of an oriental household. The dogs were the Judaizers.

Paul calls them evil workers. The term implies, not merely evil doers, but those who actually wrought against the gospel of grace. He speaks of them as the concision. The Greek word occurs only here in the New Testament. A kindred verb is used in the Greek translation of the Old Testament, speaking of mutilations forbidden by the Mosaic law such as the pagans were wont to inflict upon themselves in their religious rites (Zech. 13:4-6). The Greek word which Paul uses is a play upon the Greek word "circumcision." Paul characterizes those who were not of the true circumcision as merely mutilated. Heathen priests mutilated their own bodies. The Judaizers mutilated the message of the gospel by adding law to grace, and thus their own spiritual lives and those of their converts.

The word "worship" is the translation of the Greek word referring to the service of Jehovah by His peculiar people, the Jews. A Jew would be scandalized by the application of this word to a Gentile. Paul uses it to designate the religious service and obedience of the believer in the Church. The best Greek texts have "worship by the Spirit of God," not "worship God by the Spirit." The word "rejoice" in the Greek text has the idea of "glorying" or "exulting." It shows the high spiritual level of the apostle's life. The word "confidence" has the idea of "coming to a settled persuasion regarding something." The "we" is the editorial "we" of Paul. The implication is that the Judaizers had come to a settled confidence in the flesh, while Paul disclaims such a thing in relation to himself. Paul has used this word before in this letter (1:25). It shows that the apostle did not arrive at his decisions or convictions hastily, but only after mature consideration. Translation: *Keep a watchful eye ever upon the dogs. Keep a watchful eye ever upon the evil workers. Keep a watchful eye ever upon those who are mutilated, doing this for the purpose of bewaring of and avoiding the same. For, as for us, we are the circumcision, those who by the Spirit of God are rendering service and obedience, and who are exulting in Christ Jesus, and who have not come to a settled persuasion, trusting in the flesh.*

### Verse four

The Judaizers had confidence in the flesh. That is, they trusted in human attainments, in the works of man. Theirs was not a supernatural system in which salvation was a work of God for man, but a natural system in which salvation was a work of man for God. They did not believe in a supernatural Judaism in which God had given salvation to the offerer of the symbolic sacrifice by virtue of the merits of the coming true sacrifice for sin, the Lord Jesus. Over against this dependence of the Judaizers upon human attainment and merit, Paul sets his own human attainments and merits, saying that he had more to boast of than they, and yet he had discarded all these and any dependence upon them in order that he might appropriate the salvation which is in Christ Jesus. Thus Paul uses himself as an example to warn the Philippians against the seductive snares of the Judaizers. "Thinketh" is the translation of a word that refers to one's judgment of himself, not that of others. The word "if" refers to a fulfilled condition. There were those who did have confidence in themselves, namely, the Judaizers. Translation: *Although as for myself, I might be having confidence even in the flesh. If (as is the case) anyone else presumes to have come to a settled persuasion, trusting in the flesh, I could occupy that place, and with more reason.*

## Verses five and six

And now Paul takes inventory of those human attainments and merits in which he could trust. He says literally, "eight days old in circumcision." Converts to Judaism were circumcised in maturity, Ishmaelites in their thirteenth year. But Paul was neither. He was a pure-blooded Jew. He was "of the stock of Israel." "Of" is literally "out of," and is the word used to denote origin, the class or country of a man. The word "stock" also speaks of origin. Paul came, not from Esau but from Jacob. He belonged to the tribe of Benjamin, a tribe highly thought of, the tribe that remained loyal to David, and which formed with Judah the foundation for the restored nation after the captivities. He was the son of Hebrew parents who had retained their Hebrew language and customs, in contrast to the Hellenized Jews who read the Old Testament in the Greek language. The Greek word for "zeal" would almost have a technical meaning at that time for a strict Jew who was a member of the fanatical party among the Pharisees who called themselves Zealots. Paul had at one time considered his persecution of the Church a meritorious work. He said that he became blameless so far as the righteousness

which is in the law was concerned. He had carried this righteousness so far as to become perfect before men. Translation: *Eight
days old in circumcision, my origin, from Israelitish stock, belonging to the tribe of Benjamin, a Hebrew from true Hebrew parents,
with reference to the law, a Pharisee, with regard to zeal, a persecutor of the Church, with reference to that kind of righteousness
which is in the law, become blameless.*

### Verse seven

The word "what" in the Greek text has a qualitative aspect.
It refers to things that were of such a nature as to be an asset
or gain.  The word "gain" is plural in the Greek, namely,
"gains."  The word "those" is emphatic, namely, "these things."
"Counted" is the translation of a word meaning "to consider,
deem, think, account." It is in the perfect tense which speaks of
a process completed in past time having present results. After
mature consideration, Paul came to a settled conviction with
regard to the matter. "Loss" is singular. The various gains are
all counted as one loss. Some of the "all things" which Paul
forfeited, he has mentioned in verses five and six. Translation:
*But the things which were of such a nature as to be gains to me,
these things I have set down for the sake of Christ as a loss.*

### Verse eight

The words "yea, doubtless" are the translation of five particles,
which latter are literally translated, "yea, indeed, therefore, at
least, even," and show the force and passion of Paul's conviction.
"I count" is from the same verb that is used in verse seven, here,
in the present tense, showing continuous action in present time.
Paul had come to a settled conviction with reference to the liabil-
ity of what he termed gains, that is, when failure to appropriate
Christ would be the price he would have to pay should he hold
on to those things.  And he still held this conviction tenaciously
as an habitual attitude of his mind towards anything which

would come between him and his Lord. He still sets these things down as a loss if he by retaining them, would deprive himself of Christ.

The expression "the knowledge of Christ Jesus my Lord," does not refer to the knowledge which the Lord Jesus possesses, but the knowledge of the Lord Jesus which Paul gained through the experience of intimate companionship and communion with Him. Paul came to know His heart, His will, as one comes to know another through intimate fellowship and close association with that person. The distinctive Greek word for "knowledge" used here, leads us to this interpretation.

The expression, "for whom I have suffered the loss of all things," speaks of what Paul in his unsaved state gave up when he received the Lord Jesus as his Saviour on the road to Damascus. The words "have suffered," are in the Greek text a business term meaning, "to fine, mulct, to punish by exacting a forfeit." One could translate "for whose sake I have been caused to forfeit." Paul was a citizen of Tarsus. At the time he lived there, only families of wealth and reputation were allowed to retain their Tarsian citizenship. This throws a flood of light upon Paul's early life. He was born into a home of wealth and culture. His family were wealthy Jews living in one of the most progressive of oriental cities. All this Paul left to become a poor itinerant missionary.

But not only did he forfeit all this when he was saved, but his parents would have nothing to do with a son who had in their estimation dishonored them by becoming one of those hated, despised Christians. They had reared him in the lap of luxury, had sent him to the Jewish school of theology in Jerusalem to sit at the feet of the great Gamaliel, and had given him an excellent training in Greek culture at the University of Tarsus, a Greek school of learning. But they had now cast him off. He was still forfeiting all that he had held dear, what for? He tells us, "that I may win Christ."

This latter expression does not refer to Paul's acquisition of Christ as Saviour, but to Paul's appropriating into his life as a Christian, the perfection, the graces, the fragrance of the Person of Christ. The word "win" is the translation of the same Greek word translated "gain" in verse seven. This acquisition of the perfections of Christ, he elaborates upon in verses nine to fourteen. Translation: *Yea, indeed, therefore, at least, even, I am still setting all things down to be a loss for the sake of that which excels all others, my knowledge of Christ Jesus my Lord which I have gained through experience, for whose sake I have been caused to forfeit all things, and I am still counting them dung, in order that Christ I might gain.*

### Verse nine

The words "be found" are probably used here in a semi-technical sense found in post-classical Greek, with the meaning of "turn out actually to be." Paul uses a similar expression in Galatians 2:17, "we ourselves are found to be sinners." The idea involved is that of a revelation of character. Paul wants his life to demonstrate that he is in Christ. He wants to be found by observing men to be in Christ. The words "not having mine own righteousness," assume that Paul had a personal righteousness, which was not the case. The idea is "not having any righteousness which can be called my own." Paul did not desire to be seen to have any righteousness that would be the result of law-keeping. He was done with that. He wanted men to see in his life, the righteousness which the Holy Spirit would produce in answer to his faith in Christ. Personal righteousness in the life is referred to here rather than justifying righteousness, since only the former could be seen by men, the latter being the legal standing of the believer as in Christ and before God.

The phrase, "faith of Christ" refers to the faith which Christ kindles, of which He is the Author, which also He nourishes and maintains. It is therefore the faith which is furnished the believer by God and with which he appropriates the blessings of grace. Translation: *Yea, in order that I might through observation of others be discovered by them to be in Christ, not having as my righteousness that righteousness which is of the law, but that righteousness which is through faith in Christ, that righteousness which is from God on the basis of faith.*

## Verses ten and eleven

But Paul has forfeited the loss of all things not only that he might appropriate Christ as Saviour and have others see by his life that that was the case, but in order that he may know Him. The words "to know," are again, "to know by experience." The tense causes us to translate, "to come to know by experience." Paul wants to come to know the Lord Jesus in that fulness of experimental knowledge which is only wrought by being like Him. He wants to know also in an experiential way the power of Christ's resurrection. That is, he wants to experience the same power which raised Christ from the dead surging through his own being, overcoming sin in his life and producing the Christian graces. The Greek word for "power" used here is the same one that is used in Romans 1:16, and means, "that which overcomes resistance." He wants to come to know the fellowship of Christ's sufferings. The Greek word for "fellowship"[1] here means "a joint participation." The sufferings of Christ spoken of here are of course not His substitutionary sufferings on the Cross, but His sufferings for righteousness' sake while on earth. Paul speaks of these and of his joint-participation in them in Colossians 1:24.

When these four things are true of Paul, namely, to be discovered by men to be in Christ by the very life he lives, by coming to know Him better all the time, by experiencing the same power that raised Christ from the dead surging through his own being, and by becoming a joint-participant in His sufferings for

1. *Riches*, pp. 96-102

righteousness' sake, then Paul will constantly be made conformable to Christ's death. The words "made conformable" mean
literally, "to bring to the same form with some other person."
It is the same Greek word the apostle used in the great *Kenosis*
passage (2:5-8), meaning in its verb form "to give outward
expression of one's inner intrinsic nature." Paul's desire was
that he might so come to know his Lord, the power of His resurrection operative in his life, and a joint-participation in His
sufferings, that he would be brought to the place where he would
become, both as to his inner heart life and also as to the outward
expression of the same, like his Lord with respect to His death,
not merely His physical death which was for others, but His death
to self, as illustrated so vividly to the Philippians in the self-
emptying of the Lord Jesus in 2:7, a self-emptying that was
true of our Lord not only in His act of becoming incarnate and
of stooping to the death of the Cross, but also one that conditioned
His entire earthly life and made it the beautiful life it was, a
death to self, a denying of self for the blessing of others. This
was what Paul was striving for. The most radical conformity is
here indicated. It was not only the undergoing of a physical
death like that of Christ's, but a conformity to the spirit and
temper of His life, the meekness, lowliness, and submission of
Christ.

The expression, "if by any means" is not an expression of
doubt but one of humility. It is a modest but assured hope. "Might
attain" has the idea in the Greek text of "to arrive at, as at a goal."
The Greek word used here translated "resurrection" is only found
here in the New Testament. It is literally, "out-resurrection."

Paul is not speaking here of the future resurrection of the
physical body of the saint. That is assured him in I Corinthians
15. He has in mind the spiritual resurrection of the believing
sinner spoken of in Ephesians 2:4-8, a resurrection out from a
state in which he is dead in trespasses and sins to one in which

he is alive with the divine life of God motivating his being. Paul
desires the full operation of this life to surge through his Christian experience in such a manner that the fragrance of the life
of his Lord may permeate his life. This is the goal to which he
is striving and the goal to which he has not yet attained.

Then will be realized in his experience what he longed for in
his desire that he might be found by men to be in Christ, to have
Him as his righteousness, to come to know Him in an experiential way, to feel the power that raised Christ from the dead
surging through his being, to have a participation in His sufferings for righteousness' sake, and to be made conformable to His
death to self as spoken of in chapter 2:1-8. Translation: *Yes,
for His sake I have been caused to forfeit all things, and I count
them but dung, in order that I might come to know Him in an
experiential way, and to come to know experientially the power
of His resurrection, and a joint-participation in His sufferings,
being brought to the place where my life will radiate a likeness
to His death, if by any means I might arrive at the goal, namely,
the out-resurrection out from among those who are dead.*

## Verse twelve

In the words, "not as though I had already attained," Paul
does not have reference to a failure to attain to the out-resurrection from among those who are dead. His death or his participation in the Rapture if still alive on earth, would be the only ways
in which he could attain to this. This word "attained" in this
verse is from a different Greek word than that in the preceding
verse. In the latter instance, we found that it meant "to arrive
at, as at a goal." Here the Greek verb speaks of an active appro-
priation. That which Paul says he has not yet appropriated in
an absolute sense, he mentions in verse ten. He has come to
experience in some degree at least, the power of God surging
through his being. He has entered into a joint-participation with

Christ in suffering for righteousness' sake. The stoning at Lystra
is an example of that. He has been brought to the place in his experience where he radiates to some degree the self-lessness. the self-
abnegation of the Lord Jesus. But he has not appropriated these,
laid hold upon these, in the fullest measure. There is room for
much improvement and advance in these respects.

Then he says "either were already perfect." The Greek word
used here does not mean "sinless, flawless," but spiritually
"mature." Paul uses it three times in contrast to the Greek word
meaning spiritually "immature." The tense is the perfect. Paul
states that he has not come to the place in his Christian life where
growth in spiritual maturity has been completed, beyond which
there is no room for further development, and that as a result
he is now in a state of absolute spiritual maturity. He has not
reached a spiritual *impasse* of non-development.

The words "follow after" are from a Greek word meaning "to
pursue." He has in mind the image of a Greek runner streaking
down the race course. He is keeping up the chase, so to speak.
He is pressing on toward a fixed goal. The word "apprehend" is
from the same Greek word translated "attained," but with a
preposition prefixed which means in its local force "down." He
wants to catch hold of it and pull it down, like a football player
who not only wants to catch his man, but wants to pull him down
and make him his own. Paul wants to appropriate and make his
own that for which Christ caught Paul and made him His own.
Paul speaks of the latter in Galatians 1:16, where God's purpose
of calling Paul into salvation and the office of apostle was that
He might reveal His Son in Paul. And that is exactly what Paul
is talking about in the expression, "being made conformable to
His death." It was Christlikeness that Paul was pursuing after.
It is absolute Christlikeness that he says that he has not yet
captured and pulled down so as to make his own. Translation: *Not
that I have already made acquisition or that I have now already
been brought to that place of settled spiritual maturity beyond*

*which there is no progress, but I am pursuing onward if I may
lay hold of that for which, I have been laid hold of by Christ Jesus.*

## Verses thirteen and fourteen

The word "count" is from a Greek word which has the force
of looking back upon the process of a discussion and calmly
drawing a conclusion.   Paul had after much deliberation and
consideration arrived at the conclusions which he stated in verse
twelve.   It is evident that some of the Philippian saints had
arrived at the opposite conclusion regarding themselves, for
Paul uses the personal pronoun in the Greek in connection with
the verb here, and which, because it is not necessary as in
English to show the person of the verb, is therefore used for
emphasis and to show contrast.   The erroneous teaching of sinless perfection is not new.   It was held in the Philippian church.
The words "attained" and "apprehended" in verse twelve merely
refer to a past fact, the word "apprehend," to a present process.
But the word "apprehended" in this verse speaks of a past completed process with present results, the strongest way Paul had of
stating the fact.   That settled the question.   He meant that he
had not completely grasped that for which the Lord Jesus had
grasped him.

In the phrase "but this one thing I do," the words "this I do"
are in italics, showing that they are not in the Greek, but are
supplied by the translators.   They are not needed.   The literal
Greek here, "but one thing," sums up his Christian conduct and
purpose.   The phrase "those things which are behind," refers to
the things he had depended upon to find favor with God (3:5, 6).
"Forgetting" is stronger in the Greek, "completely forgetting."
Paul uses an illustration here of a Greek runner completely forgetting his opponents whom he is leading in the race.   Just as a
runner's speed is slackened should he think of those behind him,
and the thud, thud of their pounding feet, so the Christian's
onward progress is hindered should he dwell on the past full of

failures and sins, full of heartaches and discouragements, full of disappointments and thwarted hopes and plans. As long as a Christian has made things right with God and man, he should completely forget the past.

The words "reaching forth" are from another Greek athletic term which describes the runner whose "eye outstrips and draws onward the hand, and the hand the foot." The word means "to stretch forth after." "Press" is literally "pursue." "Mark" refers to a target for shooting, here a moral and spiritual target. "Toward" is from the preposition meaning "down," and has the idea of "bearing down upon" in the direction of the goal. The mark is Christlikeness. What a goal for a Christian! Contrast this with Omar Khayyam, "The stars are setting and the caravan starts for the dawn of nothing."

The words "the high calling" have the idea of "a calling which is from heaven and to heaven." The word is not to be construed as meaning "a calling in life," but "a call from heaven to which the apostle must ever give heed." Translation: *Brethren, as for myself, as I look back upon my life and calmly draw a conclusion, I am not counting myself yet as one who has in an absolute and complete way laid hold (of that for which I have been laid hold of by Christ Jesus); but one thing, I, in fact am forgetting completely the things that are behind, but am stretching forward to the things that are in front; bearing down upon the goal, I am pursuing on for the prize of the call from above of God which is in Christ Jesus.*

# 9.

## PAUL CLOSES HIS LETTER WITH VARIOUS EXHORTATIONS (3:15-4:23)

### Verse fifteen

PAUL says, "Let us as many as be perfect." Here he asserts that some of the Philippian saints and also he himself were perfect. But in verse twelve he denies the fact that he is yet perfect. How are we to understand this? Again, he exhorts those who are perfect, to consider themselves not yet perfect. And we ask again, how are we to understand this? Is Paul asking the Philippian saints to deny the reality of something they know to be a fact? The answer is found in the fact that in verse twelve Paul is speaking of a finished process and absolute spiritual maturity beyond which there is no room for improvement, whereas in verse fifteen he is speaking of relative spiritual maturity where there is room for development and growth. This is clear from the fact that in the former verse he uses a verb in the perfect tense, whereas in the latter, he uses a noun. Paul therefore exhorts the Philippian saints who are spiritually mature to consider themselves so only in a relative sense, and to remember that there is much room for spiritual growth in their lives. The spiritual maturity spoken of here is as we have seen, not a state of sinlessness or flawlessness, but one of completeness, of a well rounded Christian character, a state opposite to spiritual infancy.

The word "if" presents, not an hypothetical case but a fulfilled condition. Some of the Philippians were otherwise minded. Epa-

phroditus had told Paul of those in the church who were teaching sinless perfection. Paul turns these over to God. God will
reveal the truth about the matter to them if they are willing to
be taught. The word "otherwise" speaks of diversity in a bad
sense, and refers to the "otherwise" thinking of some of these
Philippian saints who thought that they had reached the place
beyond which there could be no spiritual development or progress.
Translation: *As many therefore as are spiritually mature, let us
be of this mind. And, if (as is the case), in anything you are
differently minded, and that, in an evil sense, this also will God
reveal to you.*

### Verse sixteen

The word translated "attained" is a different Greek word from
that translated "attained" in 3:12. The word there meant "to
take or appropriate." This word means "to arrive at, to reach."
It speaks of progress along a road to a certain point. Paul is
thinking of the Philippian's progress along the Christian path.
His idea is, "so far as we have come." The word "walk" means
"to proceed in a row," and refers to literal walking. Its next
meaning is "to go on prosperously, to turn out well." Then it
means "to direct one's life, to live." It has the last meaning here.
The word "rule" is not in the Greek, but has been supplied by
the translators. The literal Greek is, "walk by the same." The
context speaks of a path. Translation: *Only one thing, so far
as we have come, let us keep our lives in the same path.*

### Verse seventeen

The words "be followers together of me" could also be
rendered, "Be together, jointly, imitators of me" (Vincent) ; "Vie
with each other in imitating me" (Lightfoot). Paul is compelled
to make his own example a norm or standard of the new life. As

yet there was no tradition of the Christian life. The word "mark" is the translation of a word which means "to fix the attention upon with a desire for or interest in." It means "to observe intently." Alford offers a clearer translation for the words "mark them which walk so as ye have us for an ensample." His translation is: "mark those who walk in such manner as ye have an example in us." That is, Paul exhorts the Philippians to observe his life attentively and to become imitators of him, and to do the same also with reference to those other Christians in whose lives they find an example of Paul's own manner of life. Translation: *Become imitators of me, brethren, and observe attentively those who conduct themselves in a manner which reflects the example which you have in us.*


## Verses eighteen and nineteen

The individuals spoken of in these verses are not Judaizers but professed Christian Greeks of Epicurean tendencies. The Epicureans represented a Greek school of philosophy which taught that the satisfaction of the physical appetites was the highest aim of man. They had allowed their Christian liberty to degenerate into license (Gal. 5:13). They did not understand God's grace and thus thought lightly of continuing in sin (Rom. 6:1, 15). They were engrossed only in self-indulgence (Rom. 16:18). A swing away from legalism would land such a person into antinomianism, namely, lawlessness. Paul, acquainted with the Greek classics, writing to Greeks who knew their own literature speaks of these as having their belly as their God. He probably was thinking of the Cyclops in Euripedes who says, "My flocks which I sacrifice to no one but myself, and not to the gods, and to this my belly, the greatest of the gods: for to eat and drink each day, and to give one's self no trouble, this is the god of wise men." Translation: *For many are going about, concerning whom I often have been telling you, but now tell you weeping,*

*enemies (they are) of the cross of Christ, whose end is utter*
*destruction, whose god is their belly and that which they esteem*
*to be their glory is their shame, who regard the things upon the*
*earth.*

## Verses twenty and twenty-one

The word "conversation" is from the same Greek word which
we studied in 1:27 except that there we had the verb, and here
we have the noun.  The word here refers to the commonwealth
of which the Philippian saints of 1:27 were citizens and to which
they had citizenship obligations.  This commonwealth, Paul says,
is in heaven.  The word "is" is not the translation of the common
verb of being, but of the same Greek word found in 2:6 where
it is translated "being."  The Greek word refers to an
antecedent condition protracted into the present.  It speaks here
of fixedness.  Thus the commonwealth of which the saints are
citizens has its fixed location in heaven.  The stability and security
of the citizen under Roman law filled the thoughts of the time
with high conceptions of citizenship and its value.  Philippi,
being a Roman colony, and its citizens therefore Roman citizens,
thought in terms of citizenship.  Paul seizes this fact as a good
opportunity to illustrate to the saints their heavenly citizenship
with its privileges and responsibilities.  What a contrast between
those mentioned in 3:18, 19, who were citizens of this earth, and
those spoken of in 3:20, 21, who are citizens of heaven!

The word "look" is the translation of a Greek word made up
of three words put together, the word, "to receive," which speaks
of a welcoming or appropriating reception such as is tendered to
a friend who comes to visit one; the word "off," speaking here
of the withdrawal of one's attention from other objects, and the
word "out," used here in a perfective sense which intensifies the
already existing meaning of the word.  The composite word
speaks of an attitude of intense yearning and eager waiting for

the coming of the Lord Jesus into the air to take His Bride to heaven with Him, the attention being withdrawn from all else and concentrated upon the Lord Jesus.

The word "change" is the translation of a Greek word which speaks of an expression which is assumed from the outside, which act brings about a change of outward expression. It is the change which occurs in our physical bodies at the Rapture of the Church. These mortal bodies become immortal. These bodies which are now dominated by the soul and adjusted to its control, will be changed so as to be dominated by the human spirit, and adjusted to its control. These bodies whose life principle is now in the blood, will then be devoid of blood and will have a new life principle. These bodies of flesh and blood and bones will be bodies of flesh and bones (Luke 24:39). These bodies in whose members there resides the sin principle (Rom. 7:17, 18), will be devoid of that in their new condition. The change has to do with the body, the house or outer casing in which the person dwells. The individual himself is not changed at glorification, only his body. That is why the particular Greek word was used which denotes an outward change.

The word "vile" is the translation of the Greek word rendered "low estate" in Luke 1:48, "humiliation" in Acts 8:33, and "made low" in James 1:10. The root of the word is also found in words meaning "humble" and "humility" (I Peter 5:6; Phil. 2:8). The word "vile" today means "unclean, filthy, repulsive." When the Authorized Version was made, it meant what the Greek word means of which it is the translation, namely, "lowly, humiliated, of humble origin." These physical bodies of ours have death in them, and sickness, and weakness. The principle of sin, sometimes called the sinful nature, dwells in its members (Rom. 7:17, 18). The body has been humiliated by the fall of Adam. The enswathement of glory which proceeded out from within the inmost being of Adam before he sinned, and provided a covering of glory for his body, was taken away in the fall of man. Thus we wear clothes. The mind of Adam, functioning perfectly before the fall, was wrecked by sin. The sense functions, operating perfectly before the fall, became debilitated after he sinned. As such, our present bodies are imperfect mediums through which the regenerated Spirit-filled inner life of the believer seeks unsuccessfully to express itself in the fullest measure. The Greek work speaks of the unfitness of our present bodies to fulfil the claims of the spiritual life.

But what a transformation there will be when these bodies of our humiliation are changed so as to be fashioned like unto the body of His glory. The word "fashioned" is from the same Greek word translated "form" in 2:6, 7, which speaks of the outward expression one gives of his inner nature. A Greek preposition is prefixed which signifies a likeness to something else. Thus, this transformation of our bodies at the Rapture of the Church results in our bodies being made like our Lord's body of His glory, but not only made like it in substance and nature, but made so that they will become a perfect medium through which our inner spiritual lives can express themselves. The enswathement of glory will return. Our minds will again function perfectly. Our bodies will be immortal, perfect, free from all the effects of sin that have accumulated in 6000 years of human history.

This will all be accomplished "according to the working whereby he is able even to subdue all things unto himself." The word "working" is from a Greek word meaning "power in exercise, energy," and is only used of super-human power. The word "subdue" is the translation of a Greek military term meaning "to arrange under one's authority," as a general arranges his regiments in orderly array before himself. Thus it means here, "to bring all things within His divine economy, to marshall all things under Himself." Translation: *For the commonwealth of which we are citizens, has its fixed location in heaven, out from which, we with our attention withdrawn from all else, are eagerly*

*waiting to welcome the Saviour, the Lord Jesus Christ, and to
receive Him to ourselves: who will transform our humiliated body,
conforming it to the body of His glory, by means of the energy
through which He is able to marshal all things unto Himself.*

## Verse one

"Therefore," bearing these things in mind, living as citizens
of a heavenly commonwealth, and having a hope of a coming
Saviour, the Philippians are exhorted to stand fast in the Lord.
Paul calls them "dearly beloved." The expression is one word
in the Greek, the word which is used for God's divine and self-
sacrificial love. It is plural in number. Paul loves all of these
saints individually, and with a love produced in his heart by the
Holy Spirit. The word "longed for" is also plural. It is "divinely
loved ones and longed-for ones." The great apostle calls the
Philippian saints his crown.   The particular Greek word for
"crown"[1] here refers to the victor's garland or wreath placed upon
the head of the victor in the athletic games. It was given for
military valor. It was used at festal occasions as an expression of gladness. This garland was woven of oak leaves, ivy,
myrtle, olive, or of flowers, violets or roses. Paul's garland
of victory in his Christian service was composed of the Philippian
saints whom he had won to the Lord Jesus. Translation: *Therefore,
my brothers, individually loved ones, and individually and passionately longed for, my joy and my victor's festal garland, thus
be standing firm in the Lord, beloved ones.*

## Verse two

The apostle sends a personal word to two saints in the Philippian church. They were two women of prominence, leadership and
capability, as their names indicate. Euodia, not Euodias, which
is a man's name, means "prosperous journey." This woman in
modern language could be spoken of as "one who has arrived."

1. *Bypaths*, pp. 60-70

She has gotten somewhere in her life. Syntyche means "pleasant acquaintance, happy chance, good luck." The verb of the same stem means "to meet with." Her name indicates that she was one of those pleasant affable people who are what we call today "good mixers," one of those valuable people in the local church who is the first to greet strangers and who makes everybody feel welcome and at home. The Greek order of words is "Euodia I beseech, and Syntyche I beseech." The word "beseech" in the Greek is a strong word. It means "I exhort, I beg, please." Paul sends an individual message to each. Observe the humility and lovingkindness of the great apostle when he writes from his prison in Rome to these two women and says "please" to them, and begs them to become reconciled. He could have used his apostolic authority had he chosen to do so. Instead, in meekness and humility be beseeches. He begs them to be of the same mind in the Lord. However, this was no abrupt request. Paul had prepared these women for this exhortation in 1:27-30 where he exhorts the Philippian saints to stand fast in one spirit, and in 2:1-4, where he exhorts them all in lowliness of mind to esteem others better than themselves, and to be likeminded, in 2:5-8, where he brings to their attention the humility of the Lord Jesus, and in 2:19-30 where he speaks of the self-lessness of both Timothy and Epaphroditus. Translation: *Euodia I exhort, please, and Syntyche, I exhort, please, to be of the same mind in the Lord.*

### Verse three

The word "and" is a translation of a Greek word which assumes the granting of the request just made, and pursues the matter further. Thus does Paul suggest to these women his confidence in their willingness to comply with his request. The word "entreat" is from a word that implies a request that has back of it the authority of the apostle. When dealing with these two saints who were out of fellowship with each other because of some difference, and therefore out of fellowship with their Lord because of sin in their lives, Paul uses a very tender word, pleading with them in all humility, for one must deal very carefully with a saint out of fellowship with his Lord. Witness the "Ye which are spiritual restore such" of Galatians 6:1. It requires all the tact, love and gentleness of a Spirit-filled saint to deal with such as Euodia and Syntyche. But when Paul makes a request of the "true yokefellow," he uses his authority, for "true yokefellow," in fellowship with the Lord, is like an obedient soldier who expects just such orders given with a military curtness, and is willing to snap right into the action demanded and obey the order.

This man designated by the apostle as "true yokefellow," was a particular associate of Paul in the labor of the gospel. The word "true" refers to that which is true in the sense of genuine as contrasted to that which is counterfeit. He was "all wool and a yard wide." The word "yokefellow" is made up of a word referring to the yoke or cross-bar tied to the end of a pole and having collars or loops at each end by which two oxen were put to the plough, and a preposition meaning "with." The composite word is thought to have been used as a proper name. It was a practice among these first century Greeks at their Christian baptism, to discard their pagan name, and be given a new name descriptive of their new characters as moulded by their new Lord and Master. It was not so in the case of Diotrephes of John's third letter, whose name means "nourished by Zeus." Zeus was the principal god of the Greeks. This may indicate that the man never was saved. But Syzygus, for that is the English spelling of our Greek word meaning "yokefellow," was truly born from above, as his character and name indicated. His name referred to one who pulled well in double harness. How we need such today in our churches. What trouble-makers the "Diotrephes" kind are. To this man Paul appealed, enlisting his aid in helping these women make up their differences. He could not have appealed to a better one, for Syzygus knew how to pull well in harness with someone else, and these women did not. The word "help" implies that Euodia and Syntyche were already trying to lay aside their difficulties. The word means "to take hold with another" in a task. This same word is used where Martha asks Jesus to bid Mary lend her a helping hand (Luke 10:40). Paul asked Syzygus to lend a hand with these women in their efforts at settling their differences.

He describes Euodia and Syntyche as "those women which labored with me in the gospel." History speaks of the superior position of women in Macedonia, in which province Philippi was situated. That would account in part for the prominent place these women had in the Philippian church. The word "which" has a qualitative character. They were women who were of such a character as to have labored with Paul. The word "labored" is the translation of a Greek word used of a group of athletes who played on a team together, co-operating with one another in perfect harmony to attain a certain end, the word having in it also the ideas of strenuous and agonizing effort. This is the way Euodia and Syntyche had once worked in perfect co-operation with Paul in the great task of spreading the knowledge of the Word. But now they were causing trouble in the Philippian church, leading rival factions. The words "with Clement" are to be taken with "labored." Paul, while naming these women of distinction, did not want to imply that he had forgotten those of lesser station, Clement, and the host of other humble servants of the Lord whose names will never be heralded abroad but are nevertheless written in the book of life. Translation: *Even so, I make request of you also, Syzygus, who are a genuine yoke-fellow in deed as well as in name, lend a hand with these women in their efforts at settling the differences which they have between themselves, women of such a character that in the gospel they labored and contended in perfect co-operation with me (as a team of athletes would), together also with Clement and the rest of my fellow-workers whose names are in the book of life.*

## Verse four

*Be rejoicing in the Lord always. Again I say, be rejoicing.*

## Verse five

The word "moderation" is the translation of a Greek word having the following meanings: "not being unduly rigorous, being satisfied with less than one's due, sweet reasonableness, forbearance." The word "known" refers to knowledge gained by experience. The exhortation is therefore, "Do not keep this sweet reasonableness in your heart. Let it find expression in your conduct. Thus others will experience its blessings also." The words "at hand" are from a Greek word meaning literally "near." The nearness of the Lord's return (the Rapture is in Paul's mind), enforces gentleness and is a cure for worry. Translation: *Let your sweet reasonableness, your forbearance, your being satisfied with less than your due, become known to all men. The Lord is near.*

## Verses six and seven

The exhortation "be careful" today means, "exercise caution." When the Authorized Version was made, it meant, "be full of care." One needs to be on the lookout for words that have changed their meaning in three hundred years. The Greek word here is found in an early manuscript in the sentence, "I am writing in haste to prevent your being anxious, for I will see that you are not worried," where its translation, "anxious" is used as a synonym for the Greek word "worried." The word means "worry, anxious care." The Greek construction indicates that we have here a prohibition which forbids the continuance of an action already habitually going on. The Philippian saints were habitually worrying. Paul exhorts them to stop it. The word "nothing" is literally "not even one thing."

Then the apostle gives these saints the cure for worry, believing prayer. The word "prayer" is the translation of a Greek word which speaks of prayer addressed to God as an act of worship and devotion. "Supplication" is from a word that speaks of supplicating for one's personal needs. "Requests" is the translation of a word which emphasizes the objects asked for, namely, the things requested. The preposition "unto" in the Greek text suggests the translation, "in the presence of God," and is a delicate and suggestive way of hinting that God's presence is always there, that it is the atmosphere surrounding the Christian. Anxious care is out of place in a heavenly Father's presence. Requests are always in place with Him. The words "shall keep," are from a military word, "shall mount guard." God's peace, like a sentinel, mounts guard and patrols before the heart's door, keeping worry out. Translation: *Stop perpetually worrying about even one thing, but in everything, by prayer whose essence is that of worship and devotion, and by supplication which is a cry for your personal needs, let your requests with thanksgiving for the things asked for be made known in the presence of God, and the peace of God which surpasses all power of comprehension, shall mount guard over your hearts and minds in Christ Jesus.*

### Verse eight

We come now to a list of Christian virtues which Paul exnorts the saints to make the subject of careful reflection. The word "true" in the Greek text does not mean "truthful" in the sense of veracious, but true in character in the widest sense. "Honest" is the translation of a word which was used in classical Greek in the sense of "venerable, inviting reverence, worthy of reverence." The word exhorts here to a due appreciation of such things as produce a noble seriousness. The word "just" is from the Greek word meaning both "just" and also "righteous," here, "righteous" in a comprehensive sense. The Greek word "pure" speaks of purity in all things. "Lovely" speaks of that which is adapted to ex-

cite love and to endear him who does such things. One could translate by the words, "winsome, pleasing, amiable." The words
"good report" in the Greek text are literally "fair speaking," thus
"winning, attractive." The word "if" refers to a fulfilled condition. The word "virtue" in the Greek text was used in classical
Greek for any mental excellence, moral quality, or physical power. Paul studiously avoids it. Only here does he use it. It seems
that the apostle includes it in order that he may not omit any possible ground of appeal. Lightfoot suggests, "Whatever value may
reside in your old heathen conception of virtue, whatever consideration is due to the praise of man." *Expositor's Greek Testament*
translates, "Whatever excellence there be or fit object of praise."
The word "think" in the Greek speaks of the act of careful reflection. How scarce a commodity this is in our mechanized age.
Translation: *Finally, brethren, whatever things have the character of truth, whatever things are worthy of reverence, whatever
things are righteous, whatever things are pure, whatever things
are lovely, whatever things are attractive, whatever excellence
there be or fit object of praise, these things make the subject of
careful reflection.*

### Verse nine

The word "received" in the Greek was used regularly of receiving truth from a teacher. "Do" refers in its Greek word, to
practice as a habit. Translation: *The things also which you
learned and received and heard and saw in me, these things, habitually practice: and the God of peace shall be with you.*

### Verse ten

The words "hath flourished," are the translation of a word
found in the Greek translation of the Old Testament in the clause,
"have made the dry tree to flourish" (Ezek. 17:24). It means "to

sprout, to blossom again." Vincent translates, "Ye caused your thinking on me to bloom anew, ye revived your thought for me." Alford translates, "Ye budded forth again in caring for my interest." Expositor's offers the rendering, "You let your care for me blossom into activity again." The word "but" arrests a subject which is in danger of escaping. It was concerning the gift which the Philippians had sent by Epaphroditus. Paul had in a most delicate way thanked them in 1:3-5, using a definite article before the adverb "now," the article being a Pauline finger pointing to the gift. And while the apostle mentions the gift in so many words now, yet he is most careful in his treatment of the matter in hand, because of the base slanders that had been directed against him in the churches of Corinth and Macedonia, slanders to the effect that Paul made the gospel a means of livelihood. "Wherein" could be rendered "about whom," referring to Paul, or "in which," referring to Paul's wants. The words "were careful" are from a Greek word speaking of the act of taking thought, not from the Greek word translated "be careful" of verse six. Translation: *But I rejoiced in the Lord greatly that already once more you let your care for me blossom into activity again, in which matter you were all along thoughtful, but you never had an opportunity.*

### Verse eleven

The words "have learned" are in a construction in the Greek which speaks of entrance into a new condition. It is, "I have come to learn." Paul had not always known that. He had been reared in the lap of luxury, and had never known want as a young man. The "I" is emphatic. It is, "I, for my part, whatever others may feel." The word "therewith" is in italics and therefore not in the Greek text. It is not needed. The word "content" is the translation of a Greek word used by the Stoic school of philosophy which taught that man should be sufficient to himself for all things. It means "to be independent of external circumstances."

It speaks of self-sufficiency and competency. But Paul's self-sufficiency was not of the Stoic kind. It was Christ-sufficiency. Paul's independence was not Stoic independence, but dependence upon Christ. He found his sufficiency in Christ. He was independent of circumstances because he was dependent upon Christ. Translation: *It is not that I speak as regards want, for, so far as I am concerned, I have come to learn, in the circumstances in which I am placed, to be independent of these and self-sufficient.*

### Verses twelve and thirteen

After thanking the Philippian saints for their gift in 4:10, Paul, in view of the slanders to the effect that he was making the gospel a means of his livelihood, informs them in 4:11 that he has come to learn, in the circumstances in which he is placed, to be independent of these and self-sufficient. That being the case, he certainly is not bending any efforts at making money in gospel preaching, attempting to meet the requirements of a certain standard of life. In 4:12, he tells them that he knows how to suffer hunger and how to enjoy affluence. The words "to be abased" are the translation of the Greek word which is rendered "humbled" in 2:8, and "vile" in 3:21, and means "to make low, to humble, to humiliate." The expression refers to Paul's ability to keep himself low as respects the needs of the daily life. Paul thus assured the saints that he knew how to live on a very small income. The words "to abound" are the rendering of a Greek word which means "to overflow." Thus, Paul knew what it was to live on a little, and also to have more than he could use. The words "I am instructed" are from a technical word in the initiatory rites of the pagan mystery religions, literally, "I have been initiated," or, "I have learned the secret." The word is used in the New Testament of something which, while it may be obscure in nature or kept hidden in the past, is now revealed. The words "to be full" are from a very strong word in the original. It was

used of the feeding of animals. It means in this connection, "to
be filled," and so "to fatten like an animal." It means "to be
satiated." Translation: *I know in fact how to keep myself low;
I know in fact how to have more than enough. In everything and
in all things I have learned the secret, both to be satiated and to
be hungry, and to have more than enough and to lack. I am
strong for all things in the One who constantly infuses strength
in me.*

### Verse fourteen

The word "notwithstanding," he includes, lest in declaring his
independence of human aid, he should seem to disparage the gift
of the Philippian church. The word "well" is the translation of
the Greek word for "good" which refers to a beautiful goodness.
The phrase "ye have done well" is in the Greek the equivalent of
our present day " 'You did a beautiful thing' when you did that."
The Greek word translated "communicate" means "to make one's
self a fellow partaker in common with." The Philippians made
themselves fellow-partakers with Paul in his needs. They made
themselves responsible for the satisfying of his needs. The words
"with my affliction," tell us that it was not the actual gift so much
as the sympathy and fellowship of the Philippian saints in his
sorrow, which the great apostle valued. Translation: *All the
same, you did a beautiful thing when you made yourselves fellow-
partakers with my tribulation.*

### Verses fifteen and sixteen

The word "now" marks the transition to his first experience
of their generosity. In effect he said to them, "But this is no new
thing, for you have always been generous." Again, the word
"communicated" means "to make one's self a fellow-partaker with
someone else," and here refers to the act of the Philippians in
making themselves fellow-partakers with Paul in the responsibility

of spreading the gospel. The words "giving and receiving" are a business term referring to the credit and debit side of the ledger. The Philippian saints owed Paul much since he was the one who won them to the Lord and nurtured them in the Faith. Thus, Paul had certain credits on their ledger which they were obligated to honor. Paul referred to a like thing in I Corinthians 9:11, "If we have sown unto you spiritual things, is it a great thing if we shall reap your carnal things?" meaning by carnal things, material things. The phrase, "the beginning of the gospel," refers to the time when Paul first preached the Word to them about ten years previously. He speaks of Thessalonica, a much wealthier church. The Philippians had sent aid to Paul while he was in that city ministering to that church. Translation: *But, you yourselves also know, Philippians, that at the beginning of the gospel, when I went out from Macedonia, not even one assembly made itself a partner with me as regards an account of giving and taking except you only, that even in Thessalonica more than once you sent to relieve my necessities.*

### Verse seventeen

Paul is still defending himself against the slanderous assertion that he is using the gospel as a means of livelihood, when he says, "Not that I desire a gift." The word "desire" is in the present tense which usually indicates habitual action. Alford translates it here, "Not that it is my character or habit to seek." The word "gift" has the definite article, Paul again using it as in 1:5 to point to the particular gift which the Philippian church had just sent. The words "may abound to your account" are terms used in the money-markets of the day, namely, "interest which may accumulate to your account." Translation: *Not that it is my character to be ever seeking the gift, but I am seeking the fruit which is accumulating to your account.*

### Verse eighteen

And now Paul signs a receipt for the gift they sent him, possibly a bit of apostolic humor. The words "I have" are a rubber-stamp of the first century for, "I give you a receipt for what you sent me," or "I have received in full." The word "abound" in the Greek speaks of that which exists in superfluity. The Philippian gift must have been generous, and Epaphroditus must have been loaded down. What a demonstration of the work of the Holy Spirit is seen in this act of generosity on the part of these former pagans, performed for one who in origin, training, and religion had been and in some ways was still so different from them, different in a sense which would naturally militate against Paul, Gentiles of the proudest and most exclusive race of antiquity, the intelligentsia of the world, loving one who belonged to a race that was looked down upon and despised.

Then Paul says, "I am full." The verb is in that wonderfully descriptive Greek tense, the perfect. Paul said in this one Greek word, "I have been filled full and at present am well supplied." How the Greek language is able to compress so much into one word! The words "an odor of a sweet smell" are used in the Septuagint translation of the Old Testament, of the odors of the Levitical sacrifices. The word "sacrifice" is the Greek word used of these sacrifices. Paul wished to invest the gift of the Philippians with the sacredness of the Jewish sacrifices. Indeed, a gift to an apostle or spiritual teacher in the early Church, seems to have been regarded as an offering to God. Translation: *But I have all things to the full and overflowing. I have been filled completely full and at present am well supplied, having received at the hands of Epaphroditus the things from you, a scent of sweet savor, a sacrifice acceptable, well-pleasing to God.*

### Verses nineteen to twenty-three

Then Paul hastens to assure them that they have not impoverished themselves in giving so liberally to the cause of the gospel.

The word "supply" is the translation of the same Greek word translated "I am full." That is, God's treatment of the Philippian saints will correspond to their treatment of Paul. They filled full Paul's every need to overflowing. God will do the same for them. The measure of the supply which God the Father has is determined by His wealth in glory, which wealth in glory is in Christ Jesus, *an infinite supply*. Translation: *But my God shall satisfy to the full all your need in accordance with His wealth in glory in Christ Jesus. Now to God even our Father, be the glory forever and ever. Amen. Greet every saint in Christ Jesus. The brethren with me send greeting. All the saints send greeting, especially those of Caesar's household. The grace of the Lord Jesus Christ be with your spirit, with all of you in this respect individually.*

# INDEX OF SCRIPTURE REFERENCES

## INDEX OF SCRIPTURE REFERENCES—Continued